RIDE FOR JAKOB

Ken Smith

Dot's Micro-Publishing House
Lebanon, Kansas

RIDE FOR JAKOB

Copyright 2025 by Ken Smith

This book is an original publication of Dot's Micro-Publishing House.

All rights reserved.

No part of this book may be used or reproduced, stored in, or introduced into a retrieval system, or transmitted in any form or by any means (electronic, mechanical, photocopying, recording, or otherwise) without the prior written permission of the publisher, except in the case of brief quotations. Please refrain from participating in or encouraging the piracy of copyrighted materials that infringe on the rights of the original creator. Contact Dot's Micro-Publishing House for written permission.

Dot's Micro-Publishing House books may be purchased for educational, business, or sales promotional use at a bulk discount. For more information, please contact the Marketing Department at Dot's Micro-Publishing House.

Dot's Micro-Publishing House
29051 200 Road
Lebanon, Kansas 66952
Website: www.dotsmicropublishinghouse.com

Credits: Edited by Melanie Schlatter
Beta Read by Marion Schlatter, Jennifer Herredsberg, Denise Marcum
Vector Art by Vecteezy.com
Cover Map Created with Inkarnate.com

ISBN: 978-0-9600-8753-2 (Paperback)
SKU: 237-0-0020-2350-4 (Non-Distributed, Publisher's Copy)

Printed in the United States.

3rd Revision, 2026.

Editor's Note

This book is, at its core, a love story. It starts with a grandfather's love for his grandson, but it also includes the love of family, friends, and God. One of the key elements of Ken's purpose in writing this book is to express that love and to acknowledge the missing parts in his life, especially his wife, Jan. Though Jakob is the reason for his journey, Jan's love and support were the foundation that made the journey possible. Ken has often expressed that he wishes he could have finished the book before Jan and his daughter, Kimberley, passed away.

Beyond his purpose of expressing his love, Ken wanted this book to have an adventure-and-tour feel. Therefore, the central portion of this book explains Ken's journey. You will see pictures of the scenery from across the country, and he will occasionally delve deeper into the sights he saw. This, however, is not meant to be an exhaustive journal of his trip.

The final element of Ken's purpose is to share the importance of 'living your dream awake.' Ken has had many experiences to build on and learn from, and he wanted to share his phenomenal experience with Mannatech products. It is our hope, as Ken says, "that you will find this book inspiring and that it will instill in you the knowledge of how to be a better person and an answer to someone else's prayer."

Melanie Schlatter

Melanie Schlatter
Editor/Owner of Dot's Micro-Publishing House

PRAISE FOR *RIDE FOR JAKOB*

I'm almost finished reading Ken's book (with a box of tissues). I would love to meet him when he is here and shake the hand of someone who has so much courage and so much love in him. I believe he is one of the angels we have here on earth.

~ Eileen

The journey, as you described it in the book, seemed not only challenging but a very sacrificial journey for your grandson, who will be the recipient of all that you have achieved and sacrificed for him. Just unbelievable. Very seldom do I read a book from front to back. In this case, I couldn't put the book down without finishing it all the way through. That's an achievement for me and for you. Making this epic

journey so interesting and characteristically personal, nothing is ever done halfway by you.

~*Ubo M*

Once I started reading, I couldn't put the book down. The author takes us along on his adventure across the US and parts of Canada. It is an enjoyable and quick read.

~*Karissa S.*

the book is goated

~*S.M.*

This book will move your soul. It is not simply a diary of a grandpa who rides his bike across America. It is a love story. It is a story about dedication, passion and faith. All to support and secure the future for the author's grandson. You will not regret buying and devouring this book.

~*Amazon Customer*

Ken Smith set out to ride his bike for 3502 miles from the Atlantic to the Pacific. In mere 56 days. But this is not your average

"Adventure while traveling" book. Ken's mission is to support his grandson, Jakob, for whatever life may throw at him. What is so special about that? Jakob started experiencing severe seizures just a few days after his birth. His doctors told the family that Jakob will not live past his toddler years. Spoiler alert: Jakob is in his adult years and continues, despite still suffering from severe seizures, to live his best life. This is where Ken's story begins. He decided to ride his bike to raise awareness and funds for his grandson. During his travels, he met many interesting people who supported his cause – but he also almost lost his life on day one. Ken's diary will let you feel the deep love, dedication, and commitment he has for his grandson. Through Ken's unique writing style, you will feel every high and low of his journey and catch yourself cheering for him to not give up. This book encouraged me to take a good look at my own values and reminded myself what it means to love someone unconditionally. Ken's humble and life-loving demeanor will make you devour his book and feel like a family member. And by buying the book, you can feel even more like family since all proceeds go directly to Jakob's fund. If you read this book, you are in for a treat. You will learn more about the author himself which will leave you equally speechless.

~Janine B.

DEDICATION

This book is dedicated to my grandson, Jakob Smith, who was the inspiration for this dream to ride: bicycling from the Pacific to the Atlantic Ocean.

PART 1

THE LOVE STORY

Forward

Every dream, every goal anyone has, needs to have a PURPOSE, a REASON. Something that causes you to put ACTION into the thoughts you have. MOTIVATION to take the steps toward the VISION and DESTINATION you have created in your mind.

That initial purpose or reason has to give you what I call 'goosebumps' every time you think about it. It DRIVES you and DIRECTS you to do whatever it takes, whatever it costs you, physically, emotionally, and mentally; no matter what happens on this journey, YOU will never stop and never give up until you have achieved the GOAL and DREAM.

We are not talking about a partial achievement but the accomplishment that you know in your knower that you did the impossible and stretched your mind, body, and belief to the limit. WOW! Such a DREAM creates a feeling within YOU that you are capable of visualizing the FULL journey and gives you a sense of self-fulfillment.

It is YOURS, and even if you never speak of it or share it, the action and journey will touch others in so many ways to inspire them to birth their own dreams. What you did was the inspiration that will change their lives forever, whether you are aware of it or not.

My life experiences up to this RIDE FOR JAKOB prepared me for the ride and adventure of a lifetime. The dream was there, but I did not expect the difficulties and challenges I had to face each day - physically, but probably more so mentally and emotionally.

So, what was it that drove me to say - Just do it! My motivation was twofold: my grandson, Jakob, and my wife, Jan! Thinking of them kept me going no matter what the day brought, I would get up early every morning and go!

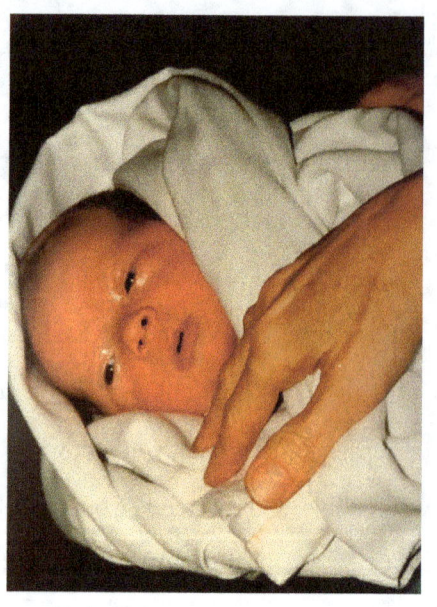

Jakob was born perfect, just like the Lord created him to be: a beautiful baby boy. I was there with Jan, on the day of his birth. It was a very meaningful day for me as I was the only son that my parents had to carry on the Smith name. Then, I had only one biological son, Jason, to carry on the Smith name, and now here comes Jakob, a son to carry on the Smith name! Talk about the excitement, joy, happiness, and sense of pride!

Then, SHOCK! Two months after Jakob's birth, he starts experiencing massive seizures. Jason and his wife, Sue, were told that because of the neurological damage these seizures had, Jakob would probably be dead by the age of 2 years old. The doctors told them he would never walk, always be in a wheelchair, and never be able to speak/talk.

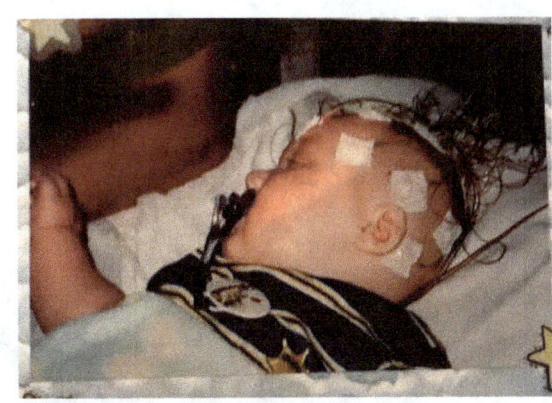

How do first-time parents handle such a diagnosis from a neurologist about their child, their first son? I could not imagine the shock and pain that my son and daughter-in-law must have felt, knowing the intensity of emotions that were going through me. No words can explain it.

Not only their shock and pain, but the disbelief of what was happening - WHY? How could this be? I know these were questions that hit me hard. When I looked at my family tree, I saw that my father was a strong, physical man, someone I looked up to. I always felt and knew I was strong physically and in good health. Then, there was my son, Jason, who was much like me in many respects. Therefore, you just expected and believed that this trend would continue. So, why wouldn't it? What happened?

All the plans that had been made were now called into question. Life would be different for everyone, especially for my son and daughter-in-law, and even in the years ahead, as Jason and Sue had another child, my granddaughter, Brooklynn Smith.

THE SMITH FAMILY PICTURE:

Jason, Sue, Jakob, Brooklynn

Jakob is now 23 years old, and Brooklynn's life will be different, as well, as she is faced with caring for a brother who needs special care for the rest of his life.

Having Jakob is such a blessing, and yet, it is a commitment that has changed us all forever! Seeing all that goes into his care changes how you think, how you live, and how you care for others. I admire this family for what they have done for Jakob and the love that all 3 of them have instilled in their home, making Jakob's life the best he could ever imagine. Jakob is BLESSED, and so are all of us!

I believe Jakob's life and his story will touch the lives of anyone and everyone he encounters. You cannot help but want to love on him and hug him because you know and feel you are now a part of his life. You just have to meet him, and I hope you all do someday.

JAKOB'S EARLY STORY BY SUE SMITH
Jakob's mother, Written 2004

Jakob had what I thought was a daydream sometime between February and June 2002. What started as a daydream quickly turned into watery eyes, purple lips, gagging reflexes, and screaming episodes. We soon found out that Jakob was having seizures. The seizures lasted up to a minute in length, and he would have 6-8 a day. It was such a scary time for Jason and me as there were so many unanswered questions. On June 24, 2002, Jakob had his first EEG to confirm the seizures. On June 27, 2002, we were quickly rushed into to see the neurologist Dr. Levine, who informed us that it did not look good for our little guy. We asked what our future would hold for Jakob and he said that best case Jakob would need a wheelchair or worst-case Jakob might die before he was two. Jason had to lie on the ground and my mom took Jakob as I could not contain my emotions. To hear that your child might not live was the hardest thing to ever hear; it ripped out my heart. It was on the way home that God filled my heart with an unexplainable peace, letting me know Jakob would be fine. Jakob is now 2 years and 4 months old and doing better than ever. He has been seizure-free for almost a year and will be walking very soon. All of the tests have shown nothing, so we live without a diagnosis. However, we live with such hope seeing Jakob progress every day. If nothing else, we can learn through Jakob's story that there is one person in charge of our lives and that is God.

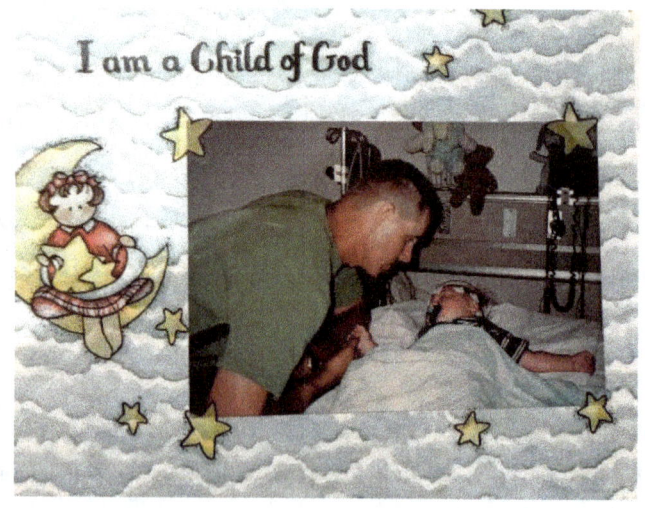

Speechless by Brooklyn Smith

Jakob's sister

I'm speechless.

I wake up I have no words.

I go to school I have no words.

I try to communicate with other people but I have no words!

I'm speechless.

I want to tell my family how much I love them but I can't.

I really hope they know that I do.

I hit my head to try and tell them something but they put a helmet on me because they don't understand!

I also have a bad habit of pinching but I just have so many words, thoughts, and so much more that I need to say but I can't.

I'm speechless.

There is one good thing though.

Even though sometimes I feel like the only one, 25% of people in the world are like me.

Also, I know my family really loves me and will do anything for me.

I'm Jakob, this is my life.

I'm speechless.

MOTIVATION

So, what started the DREAM of RIDE FOR JAKOB?

It was Christmas 2017 when Jan and I went to visit Jason, Sue, and the family in Canada. Jason is a firefighter and follows in the footsteps of my father in that degree. When we are together, we often discuss his job and the things he has had to do, many of which are truthfully dangerous.

THE EXTENDED SMITH FAMILY PICTURE

Jason, Grandpa Ken, Sue,
Great Grandma Smith, Jakob, Brooklynn, Grandma Jan

2017

I was watching Jakob, and it HIT me - what is going to happen to Jakob *IF* anything were to happen to Jason or, for that matter, both my son and daughter-in-law? Who is going to look after him? There was no one in the family on either side that was in a position to take Jakob and, for that matter, Brooklynn, as well.

Did Jason and Sue have anyone in mind? I did not know. But the question weighed heavily on my heart and mind and wouldn't ease up: What is going to happen to Jakob?

So, I decided I needed to ask Jason. "What plans have you made for Jakob's unknown future?" The answer was, "Jakob will be with us for as long as he lives or as long as we live." But still, the future for any of us is 'unknown-uncertain.' Jason confessed: "Dad, I don't know. You can't take a child who has had a loving family taking care of him every day as we have and put him into a home or a foreign environment where he knows NO ONE for the rest of his life." This HIT me and HURT so much that I felt compelled to do something, ANYTHING, that could make a difference for Jakob's future security.

It brought me to tears thinking how a child who has known nothing other than a loving, caring family environment could be forced into an institutionalized home. I am not saying an institutionalized home is not a good place; it simply could not compare to having the loving environment of a home. It's questionable that any home other than his own would give him the care, love, and relationship he has with my son and daughter-in-law. I couldn't live with myself thinking I was going to sit by and watch his life unfold like that and do nothing. I couldn't do it.

That is when RIDE FOR JAKOB was born. I envisioned riding my bike from the Pacific Ocean to the Atlantic Ocean and implementing a fundraising program to raise money for Jakob's future security. I had no idea how I was going to do this, but I knew it was going to happen. As his grandfather, I knew I could make a difference for my grandson, one way or another.

My wife, Jan Smith

My biggest supporter and the love of my life was my wife, Jan. Jan developed breast cancer in 2015. Yet, she knew the DREAM and

the WHY for taking this RIDE FOR JAKOB adventure. The words I heard Jan say most often regarding this dream were---GO FOR IT!

She knew the potential risk I was going to encounter. Still, she also came from the same mindset and background of having a positive attitude, being a high achiever, and setting an example of 'never give up', no matter what you encounter or what life circumstances throw at you. Jan's words of encouragement were also this: LIFE IS A DARING ADVENTURE IF NOTHING AT ALL!

Just knowing that I was going to be gone for at least 2 months (60 days) would be an incredible emotional strain because of her condition, but Jan also knew the love that we both shared for Jakob and his family. She also knew this was important to me and would be the ride of a lifetime, one I may never be able to do again, so she'd say, "Just go for it!"

During the journey, her daily calls continued to lift me up. Her many prayers of protective covering were so vital and important to me as I encountered many potential situations that could have turned out quite differently. I knew it had to be her spiritual covering that put angels before me, behind me, and protected me.

Jan passed away in October 2021, just 20 days after our daughter, Kimberley, both from a valiant fight with breast cancer. I simply cannot express the impact these losses had on me. I have a few tributes to Jan at the back of this book.

"YOU NEVER KNOW HOW STRONG YOU ARE UNTIL BEING STRONG IS THE ONLY CHOICE YOU HAVE"

When putting this book together, the only wish that I had was that I would have been able to finish it and the adventure before my beloved Jan passed away. Jan always said: I had a dream one night where I saw Jakob look at me and say - HI GRANDMA!

...AND THAT DAY WILL COME!...

My RIDE FOR JAKOB, regardless of the demand on my body and the risks and challenges I faced, would be worth it. I love this little guy, and I will always know in my heart that I did something for him. He may never know, but I will, and God will.

There are so many people, young and old, who have been afflicted with a neurological condition. Who knows why, but when it touches someone in your family as a child, your heart breaks, and all you can do is PRAY daily for them. But for me, I wanted to do more.

When you think about it, we have so much, and for those of us who are blessed with somewhat good health, we can create a future for ourselves, but children like Jakob have NO knowledge of what the future is going to be like. I needed to know that I did something that would help make his future more secure and comfortable.

GRANDPA RIDES FOR JAKOB

(adapted from the poster created to promote awareness)

If Jakob could talk, I believe he would say something like this…Hi, my name is Jakob Smith. Shortly after my birth, I began having 6-8 seizures a day. The neurologist informed my parents that it did not look good for me: I would probably never be able to speak, I would be confined to a wheelchair, and I would probably die before I turned 2.

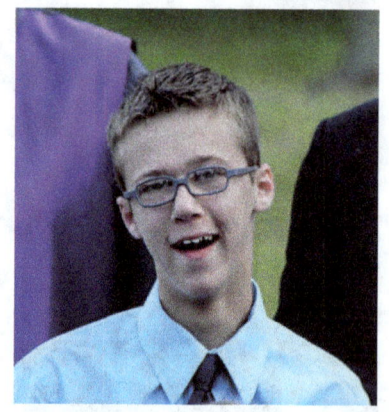

However, God is so AWESOME! I turned 23 on January 24, 2025, and have never needed a wheelchair. I am unable to speak and do need around-the-clock care because of neurological damage. But I have a loving family, and my life is good.

My grandpa, Ken Smith, at the age of 70, embarked on a bicycle ride across America from the Pacific to the Atlantic Ocean, traveling 3502 miles in just 56 days to raise money for my inflating medical costs and future care. This ride took place in July, August, and September of 2018.

He encountered many challenges from extreme heat, mountains, near-death accidents, fatigue, miles with no cell phone connections, and exhaustion, yet he ACCOMPLISHED this all for me. Even though I cannot express my feelings, I want my grandpa to know: 'I LOVE HIM and THANK HIM for all he has done for me!"

Jakob

Jakob & Ken

JAKOB NOW

Jakob recently graduated high school. Each year, we saw how he engaged with other children who loved him, played with him, and treated him with kindness and laughter. This interaction with people over the years is evident in how Jakob engages with new people and reacts when we visit.

Now that Jason and Sue work more consistently, Jakob attends a day facility. Jakob loves sports, and in the winter, one of his favorite things to do is snow ski. Jason takes him almost every day that the slope is open and his work allows. Isn't it amazing how this young man who wasn't even supposed to be able to walk can ski?!

As mentioned, Jakob is now in his twenties and still needs daily care. This does not mean that he sits around doing nothing all day. Jason and Sue make sure that Jakob has plenty of socialization and as full a life as he is able to live. Following are several pictures of Jakob living life to the fullest.

JAKOB

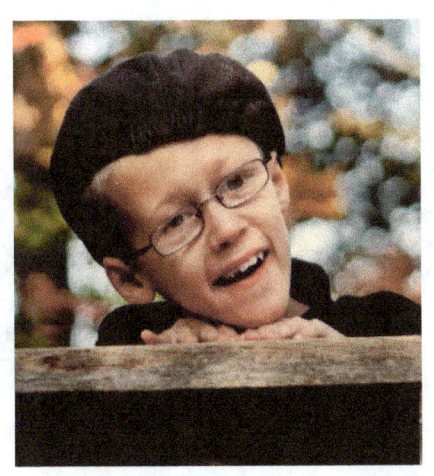

Jakob & Jason

Jakob & Sue

JAKOB & BROOKLYN

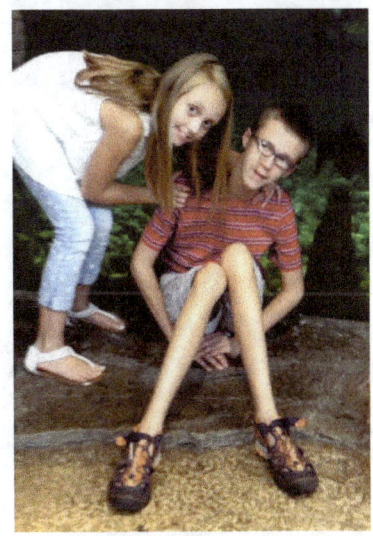

LIVING THE GOOD LIFE

PART 2

THE ADVENTURE

How it Started

In 2015, I met a father and son duo who had ridden their bikes to our church one morning. I had previously done a few triathlons and thought I'd strike up a conversation with these guys to find out what they were up to. As it turns out, they were riding from the Pacific to the Atlantic, and Grand Rapids was a stop along the way. As I walked away from them, I thought, 'One day, I'd like to do that!'

Fast forward to 2017, our visit to Canada, and my revelation that I needed to do something to help provide for Jakob's future. I began looking into how to make a RIDE FOR JAKOB happen.

I met another man, Jim Meyers, who had ridden the Southern tier of the Pacific to Atlantic routes established with the Adventure Cycling Association out of Missoula, Montana. After talking with him, he decided he'd like to do it again on the Northern tier. We followed the Route Maps provided by the Adventure Cycling Association out of Missoula, MT. Having someone who had done a ride like this before, as well as having the routes established by a known resource, gave me peace of mind.

As I planned my ride, I decided that having what cyclists call a 'sag wagon' or pace car was not needed. My daughter would track me with her Life360 app, and I felt perfectly safe with the known route and the frequent stops we would be making.

Route

Day	Start	End	Miles	Total
1	Seaside, OR	Clatskanie, OR	65	65
2	Clatskanie, OR	Portland, OR	73	138
3	Portland, OR	Hood River, OR	73	211
4	Hood River, OR	Biggs Junction, OR	40	251
5	Biggs, Junction, OR	Umatilla, OR	80	331
6	Umatilla, OR	Walla Walla, WA	55	386
7	Walla Walla, WA	Pomeroy, WA	65	451
8	Pomeroy, WA	Lewiston, ID	35	486
9	Lewiston, ID	Orofino, ID	35	521
10	Orofino, ID	Lowell, ID	57	578
11	Lowell, ID	Lolo Pass, MT	86	664
12	Lolo Pass, MT	Missoula, MT	43	707
13	Rest Day in Missoula, MT			
14	Missoula, MT	Lincoln, MT	73	780
15	Lincoln, MT	Great Falls, MT	97	877
16	Great Falls, MT	Lewistown, MT	105	982
17	Lewistown, MT	Winnett, MT	52	1034
18	Winnett, MT	Jordon, MT	75	1109
19	Jordon, MT	Circle, MT	67	1176

ROUTE CONTINUED

Day	Start	End	Miles	Total
20	Circle, MT	Glendive, MT	45	1221
21	Glendive, MT	Medora, ND	65	1286
22	Medora, ND	Hebron, ND	77	1363
23	Hebron, ND	Bismarck, ND	55	1418
24	Bismarck, ND	Jamestown, ND	105	1523
25	Jamestown, ND	Fargo, ND	94	1617
26	Rest Day in Fargo, ND			
27	Fargo, ND	Fergus Falls, MN	81	1698
28	Fergus Falls, MN	Melrose, MN	85	1783
29	Melrose, MN	Milaca, MN	70	1853
30	Milaca, MN	St. Croix Falls, WI	74	1927
31	St. Croix Falls, WI	Red Wing, MN	74	2001
32	Red Wing, MN	Winona, MN	73	2074
33	Winona, MN	Kendall, WI	73	2147
34	Kendall, WI	Sauk City, WI	65	2212
35	Sauk City, WI	Johnson Creek, WI	65	2277
36	Johnson Creek, WI	Milwaukee, WI	61	2338
	Ferry over to Muskegon, MI			
37	Muskegon, MI	Kentwood, MI	61	2399
	Anniversary Break with Jan			
38	Grand Rapids, MI	St. Johns, MI	61	2460

Route Continued

Day	Start	End	Miles	Total
39	St. Johns, MI	Flint, MI	53	2513
40	Flint, MI	Wallaceburg, ON	52	2565
41	Wallaceburg, ON	Jason & Jakob Picked Me Up		
42	Longwood, ON	London, ON	41	2606
43	Rest Day in London, ON			
44	London, ON	Simcoe, ON	65	2671
45	Simcoe, ON	Dunnville, ON	51	2722
46	Dunnville, ON	Fort Erie, ON	47	2769
47	Fort Erie, ON	Albion, NY	76	2845
48	Albion, NY	Palmyra, NY	68	2913
49	Palmyra, NY	Syracuse, NY	76	2989
50	Syracuse, NY	Utica, NY	75	3064
51	Utica, NY	Schenectady, NY	84	3148
52	Schenectady, NY	Troy, NY	23	3171
53	Troy, NY	Florida, MA	50	3221
54	Florida, MA	Boston, MA	62	3283
55	Boston, MA	Boston East Hotel	45	3328
56	Boston East Hotel	Revere, MA	20	3348

When my front tire touched the Atlantic Ocean, my odometer read 3502. The additional 154 miles are miles I rode my bike for supplies, touring, and meals along the route.

Now, I needed a bike. I went to a bike shop in Grand Rapids called Freewheeler Bike Shop. They were great. After explaining what I was doing, the owner highly suggested that I purchase a steel-framed touring bike. These bikes are heavier than a normal road bike and are made to carry four bags. The tires were larger but not as wide as those of a mountain bike, so they could handle the rougher off-road conditions of rail trails when needed.

To customize the bike, they mounted it on a stand so I could sit on it stationary. They had a computer program that calculated all the adjustments needed for the bike to fit my body structure. They could adjust the seat by measuring my leg length, so I had a full leg extension. Then, they took my arm length and height to adjust the handlebars to reduce the lower back stress. They even suggested a proper seat that enabled my butt and hips to fit comfortably on the bike. I am sure glad they recommended the customization; it would be a long ride for an ill-fitted bike.

The Bike Shop also hooked me up with supplies, donated shirts, bags, and other equipment to help cut down on the cost of the ride. As mentioned before, my bike could carry four pannier bags. I filled them with jeans, good pants, extra shirts, food bars, running shoes, sandals, a heavier coat for the mountains, vitamin and mineral supplements, suntan lotion, underclothes, towels, toiletries, first aid and repair items, and PJs. Eventually, I added a light tent and roll-up mattress.

After I had my bike, Jim called one day, "Want to go for a ride?"

I was like, "Sure, I need to get used to my bike."

We went for a 25-mile ride. That was the one and only ride we took before we headed for Seaside, Oregon, to start our journey in July 2018.

Since this was supposed to be about raising funds for Jakob, I talked to everyone I could think of about my ride. I had a GoFundMe link to help facilitate donations. (That link is no longer active.) Various friends and family helped get the word out using a brochure I had made. I also gave a few speeches at a convention and did phone meetings. I had signs on my bike that led people to stop and ask questions. Various TV and radio stations also asked for interviews.

The biggest connection I made was with the International Association of Fire Fighters (IAFF). With both my father and my son being firefighters, I decided to stop by the local fire department to see if they would be interested in supporting this cause. I knew that various Fire Fighters Associations encouraged this kind of involvement.

Fire Inspector Bill Smith took my RIDE FOR JAKOB brochure to the Fire Chief of Grand Rapids. The Fire Chief wrote a letter of recommendation stating what I was doing, vouching for me as being legit, and asking for support from any fire station I went to for help. This started the entire firefighter support program that opened doors for us across the nation. When it worked out, my sister Lois would even call ahead to the fire stations to see if they could assist me along the way. Though I never knew what to expect, the outpouring of support from the fire stations was overwhelming.

A few of the Fire Stations I stopped at:

Seaside, OR

Portland, OR

Umatilla, OR

Grand Rapids, MI

Wallaceburg, ON

Albany, NY

Delaware, ON

Lewiston, ID

Many stations we stopped at were volunteer-only, did not have accommodations, or were not manned 24-7. Those stations are just as important but were not on the list of ones we visited. I apologize if I missed any; please know you were ALL appreciated!

Although we followed the route maps, MANY roads had no shoulder to ride on, making things much more dangerous. On the next page is a map with the path I took highlighted, followed by a recount of the daily journey from both the Facebook page and my recollections from 2018.

Day 1

Tuesday, July 24; Seaside, OR to Clatskanie, OR; Daily Miles 65. The first day was motivating. The Seaside Fire Department gave us a great send-off. I appreciated their interest, excitement, and encouragement for this ride.

Pacific Ocean, Seaside, Oregon

Jim & Ken at the start of their journey.

Seaside Fire Department

I was told the coastal mountains were going to be a tough ride, and they were right. Their *looooong* climbs were truly a test of endurance. There were a couple I just couldn't conquer on my bike, so I had to walk to the top. One of them was some 4 miles long. I just couldn't do it.

I really had very little pre-riding experience with this bike, and I was a little uncomfortable in changing gears. I now know I should have taken more time to ride and train with the bike.

I was not expecting the coastal mountains to be so challenging, especially right from the beginning, and almost immediately after we left Seaside. My riding partner, a more experienced biker, was miles ahead of me. That being said, I realized that I would be making this ride for the most part—ALONE.

Another challenge for this first day was the falls. Two falls on the 1st day! I was not expecting this. My first fall was actually a near rear-end hit by a logging truck. I knew this road was being used by logging trucks, as there were many signs posted along the highway. I was riding on a flat, straight part of the highway, approaching a sharp left turn. I took advantage of the lane because of the sparse traffic I encountered. As I approached this turn, I heard the logging truck downshifting, and I knew he was approaching me very quickly. I started to ride faster to get around the curve, only to find that it was a long, uphill, narrow road and, again, nowhere to pull over for the truck to pass. I knew he was close based on the sound of his downshifting and the sound of his horn. He must have felt he was going to hit me because I could not get out of his lane. I turned my head to look behind me, and I noticed that his front bumper was just inches from my back fender. I just knew I was going to be hit (and this was day 1.) That being said, I did the only thing I could do, which was to make a fast turn and ride into the ditch.

When I came to a rest, I realized it was so very close to being a tragedy that I just laid there thinking about what had happened. The logger really could not have moved over to the passing lane as the road was too narrow, and it was a steep uphill climb for him. He also would not have known if there was going to be any oncoming traffic coming down and around the corner. Coming to a stop wasn't an option as he had a full load of logs and obviously didn't see me on the road until it was too late. That being said, he didn't stop to see if I was OK. He just kept going.

The second fall was a big one. I couldn't release my clip-on shoe fast enough and lost my balance. I did get a nasty cut on my left leg and knee, broke my mirror, scratched my legs and arms, and had a bad bruise on my hip that I noticed at the end of the day. Other than that, I had no other issues with my bike - thank God. Wrecking my bike on day one would have been a bad way to start my ride across America.

This was a tough first day! It was a long HOT day, and pushing my bike up those long mountain roads was not easy, especially since I had four riding saddles, two on the front wheel and two on the back. I had far too much weight for doing these mountain rides, with just over 100 pounds that I had to push for hours uphill. All in all, I was tired at the end of the 60 miles, but I could have gone further if it weren't for the extreme mountain climbs. I was so looking forward to getting to the motel that day.

Now, here is something I want to make note of. I did train to some degree for this ride across the U.S., or it would not have been possible. In my training schedule, I did a lot of weight lifting, running, and climbing the high school football stadium stairs, some 1100 in total, almost every day for weeks. Regardless of what nutritional supplement I had taken during my training, I always knew

I had had a good training day because my legs and body felt it. By this I mean, stiffness and sore muscles were common, especially a few hours after the strenuous exercise or the next morning.

Therefore, after the first day's 60 miles and what I experienced, I was expecting the same results, but it did not happen. That evening and the next morning, nothing, no stiffness or soreness. "What's this?" I asked myself.

The ONLY thing that I took that was different from the past products was those that I received from Mannatech. "Do these Mannatech products work that well?" WOW, I was impressed. So, let's just see what happens tomorrow.

Let me just say - I slept very well that night! But I knew we would be up and riding again by 8 a.m. the next morning at the latest. We tried to keep a daily routine: Up by 7 a.m., have breakfast, say a prayer for protection, get on the road, arrive at our destination, get supper, wash riding top and shorts, hang them to dry, head to bed, wake up, and repeat.

Day 2

Wednesday, July 25; Clatskanie, OR to Portland, OR; Daily Miles 73; Total Miles 138. Today was a day full of BLESSINGS! No major issues along the ride other than it was 95 degrees. HOT!

The day started at Clatskanie, Oregon. It was an overcast day, to begin with, but it sure got HOT fast. Day 2, and I decided that I had better carry more water. We really didn't have a challenge in getting extra water as we needed it simply because there were a number of stores, gas stations, and restaurants along the route. Since the water got hot fast in my containers, at each refill, I filled them with as much ice as I could.

We knew we had a long mountain to climb, but the receptionist at our motel showed us a way to route around Highway 30 that had a number of hills to climb but nowhere near the ones we would experience if we stayed on the main highway. As I rode along the highway, I stopped at a fruit stand to get a peach. The lady saw my sign about Jakob and my ride across America. She gave me the peach and said, 'That is the least I can give you. Safe riding.'

Next, I stopped at a Subway for a quick lunch. Again, a woman saw my sign and offered to buy my lunch. Then, I came to a very busy highway that crossed a bridge into Portland and was forced to walk alongside the cars and trucks. A guy pulled over ahead of me and gave me a donation. Several people opened their windows and said, 'Keep safe,' and I got many 'thumbs up' signs. I stopped at a bike shop and had my bike serviced. It needed it. Jim had a flat tire, the first of 7 flats while we were together.

I called the local fire chief and introduced myself and explained what I was doing. I shared the story about Jakob. He called the Grand Rapids Fire Department and checked us out. They apparently said I was the real deal! I just have to say a few words about the Portland Fire Department. These guys were great. The meal they gave us was wonderful, and they offered a room for the night at one of the fire stations. In the morning, there was a new crew, and they made breakfast for us as well.

That's the kind of organization the IAFF is. We couldn't thank them enough for their hospitality.

Each morning after breakfast, Jim set our final destination for the day and then he was off and riding. At times, he was not only miles ahead of me but hours as well. He gave me some great advice on how to fix my bike in case of a breakdown, but that being said, I was on my own most of the time. With my past of risk-taking, I never really let it bother me (you can read about those experiences in the back of the book).

For me, each turn in the road and each mountain to climb was a new experience and challenge. I loved it! This private time (hours) actually enabled me to think about my life, where it was going, what I could do for Jakob and his family, how I could make a difference in the lives of others, etc., etc., etc. Also, I prayed a lot for safety and protection, not only for me but also a prayer covering for Jan while I was away.

This was only day 2. I had no idea how long this ride was going to be, but in just these 2 days, I underestimated the challenges in front of me. The heat was something that I did not expect, and I came to realize that I had far too much baggage, which was just too much to carry and push. My shoes were not made for walking as they were riding shoes, and that just made it a little more difficult, especially pushing the bike up the mountain roads.

I carried Jakob's picture on my carriage bag between my handlebars throughout the ride. Whenever I felt especially challenged or alone, I would take the time to focus on Jakob's picture. That was all I needed to keep me going. I had a goal and a purpose. Thank you, Jakie! That night, I crashed again at 9:00 p.m. but was ready for the next day.

> **Thoughts for the Day:** Hmm, interesting. I'm experiencing something that's hard to express. Yes, I'm tired, which I expected. After two days of riding, I'm surprised by the absence of sore muscles, and I've been anticipating the physical CRASH! So far, nothing. It must be the Mannatech products. Let's see what happens tomorrow.

DAY 3

Thursday, July 26; Portland, OR to Hood River, OR; Daily Miles 73; Total Miles 211. The day started out great. In the morning, I had a newspaper interview in Portland, and he was excited about the reason for my RIDE FOR JAKOB. The temperature was 91 degrees.

As I left Portland, a local newspaper called me, and they asked if I could give them an interview over the phone. They were contacted by my sister, Lois, who was so instrumental in connecting me with the press, radio, TV, fire, and police departments. This just gave me a greater sense of peace and safety, knowing I was being watched or that I could call someone at any time for help. My sister was a real blessing. I called her my 'eyes in the sky' or my 'air traffic controller.' I just felt safe knowing she was going before me. For the most part, riding through Portland and most cities was somewhat confusing.

You really needed GPS and good maps to know where to turn or what direction you needed to go. The maps we got were to some degree helpful, but you really had to read them closely to know what direction to go.

As I rode and reflected, this difficulty in finding direction and knowing where to go made me think of the early years of Jakob's life. There were so many things that happened unexpectedly. Jason and Sue had to learn how to recognize the onset of a seizure, what medications were needed when, and I'm certain many times the road

was not always evident before them. Sometimes, there were wrong turns, just like what happened to me on this ride, because what I was seeing wasn't the same thing I saw on my map. At those times on my ride, people showed up and offered to help. They rode along with me, gave me a ride, or just set me in the right direction. How many people did that for Jason and Sue? How can I still do that for them or others?

I had an opportunity to stop and help two women with a flat tire. They didn't know how to change the tire, so I offered to help. It was HOT! The first 40 miles were okay, but riding along the highway was an experience with heavy traffic, and I had to make a detour due to construction.

The detour was not expected. My riding partner had already left me and was miles ahead of me at this time. I called and asked what route he went on, and he informed me that I had to follow the detour through the backcountry. I have to say this was somewhat of a scary ride. I was in the deep forest, there were NO houses or any sign of human occupation. I started to think of mountain lions or (this is stupid - BIG FOOT!) You know the stories about this part of the Oregon rainforest area.

Believe me, it was lonely and dark in many areas, but the streams and wooded country were beautiful. I was seeing a part of America that I think few people really see who stick to the interstate highways or main roads. I have to say I found this exciting and a great adventure doing this alone. Oh, by the way, there was NO cell phone connection to the outside world on this detoured route.

One experience I had on this route was when I had to go through a mountain tunnel. It was dark, with about a 2-foot shoulder to the wall. The traffic was heavy, especially with semis. I didn't want to ride through it, so I walked. Not really a good idea. My riding top was black, and they couldn't see me, but I made it.

What made this day difficult was the elevation and curvy mountain roads. I just kept wondering, each time I reached the top of the road or the next turn, that I was at the end of this climb and was now going to go downhill. I had to walk some 6 miles all uphill, pushing my bike and gear with riding shoes not meant for walking.

I enjoyed the shade and coolness of the forest, but the temperature for the day was over 100 degrees again. I decided that as soon as I could downsize my gear, etc. I was going to have only two bags vs. the current four.

I finally reached the top and was excited for the ride downhill. I don't know what was worse, though, walking uphill or riding downhill on a winding road with a 10-degree decline for some 5 miles. I rode my brakes the whole distance, and they were HOT, believe me.

It took me a few more miles before I reached Hood River, Oregon, and caught up with my riding partner. I have to say I did not feel quite as alone compared to Day 1, as I faced all the issues and experiences on my own. I just knew that whatever happened, happens, and I'd just have to deal with it.

Again, it was like 'living on the edge' and never knowing what was going to happen. For some, I guess that would scare them, but I've been here before, like when I was in the Amazon Jungle *(About the Author, p. 211)*. So, I kept telling

myself, "Life is a daring adventure or nothing at all. Just deal with it, Ken, and keep going." That's the statement Jan would say all the time. I loved it!

It was a long day, and I was sore with a few muscle cramps during the ride, but overall, it was a successful day. Tomorrow night, we will be in Biggs, Oregon.

> **Thoughts for the Day:** I experienced a few muscle cramps, which was expected – I came to realize that I hadn't drunk enough water today. Nothing serious going on physically to prevent me from going on. Again, I'm left thinking, "Let's see what tomorrow morning brings."

DAY 4

Friday, July 27; Hood River, OR to Biggs Junction, OR; Daily Miles 40; Total Miles 251.

We left Hood River early in the morning at 8:00 a.m. We planned to get up and have breakfast as early as possible every day simply because of the heat. We made sure we had sunscreen on and proper light leg cover-ups. I already had some sunburn, but not bad. If this day was going to be like the past few days, then the temperature was going to hit the 100-degree marker again.

Our goal today was to get 40 miles to Biggs Junction, Oregon. The ride along Highway 84 was very scenic as it went along the Columbia River. Again, a mountainous area. I could not believe the number of mountain ranges there were from the coastal mountains to the Rocky Mountains. I was able to ride most of the time, but then again, the odd mountain climbs sure took their toll.

We arrived at The Delles City, a city on the route, and it was a well-earned rest for an hour or so. We found a bike shop as we entered the town. I made sure that whenever there was a bike shop, I was going to get my bike serviced. I never had any issues with my tires, but my cable and chain needed adjusting and lubricating.

The owner of the bike shop was impressed with my ride commitment and donated his time for servicing my bike and gave to the RIDE FOR JAKOB fund. Cool! He also told us to drive with care as the traffic this time of the year was especially heavy with a lot of vacationers, trucks, trailers, etc.

At times, there were no guard rails either, and you were able to look down the side of the highway with a steep slope to a river flowing below. You literally could not ride past the white line if there was one, so almost all riding was on the main highway. Somewhat unnerving at times. It's a pretty awesome country, but you had to be constantly watching passing vehicles.

We arrived at Biggs Junction at about 4:00 p.m. in the afternoon. It was time to stop. Biggs Junction was just a small town along the Interstate if you call it that. I found an ice cream store and just pigged out. Loved it! We always found a small restaurant each evening, and I must say, we ate! Or at least I did. Now ready for a shower and bed shortly after that.

> **Thoughts for the Day:** Today was a great day of riding. I made sure to drink plenty of water with my supplements and throughout the day. It's interesting; with all the water I consumed, I really didn't have to stop to pee any more than usual, which wasn't what I expected. I probably need to be vigilant to avoid getting dehydrated.

Day 5

Saturday, July 28; Biggs Junction, OR to Umatilla, OR; Daily Miles 80; Total Miles 331.

We left Biggs Junction at 8:00 a.m., knowing the day was going to be another scorcher (HOT). We initially thought we would experience somewhat moderate temperatures, but this was not the case. For me, it turned out to be my worst day of riding ever!

We had two choices regarding the highway we should take: keep to the Oregon side of the river, which appeared to be very busy or cross over to the Washington side, which had less traffic but was on a higher level.

Looking at the highway across the river from the motel, it is evident that the first part of the day was a very long uphill ride on a highway with a few curves to get to the top before it leveled off. I watched a few semis move along very slowly because the climb and elevation were steep.

So, we decided to cross the Columbia River to the Washington side. Bad decision for me! I had to walk most of the highway to the top. I rode a lot of it, but I wasn't all that familiar with the gearing on my bike, so I basically stayed in the few gears that I was comfortable with.

I traveled for several hours and used up most of my water. The Mannatech Empact+ I mixed up got hot in the bottle. I mean, really hot! My throat was so irritated it was difficult to swallow the hot liquid. Once, I was forced to buy a Gatorade, and it got too hot as well, hurting my throat and upsetting my stomach. After that, I stuck with the Empact+ only, and with the little sticks they came in, I could mix them when I got fresh water! So, each stop I made, I would mix up some Empact+, rest while I drank it, and then get back on the road. It made a huge difference.

After 60 miles, I had to stop as I ran out of water and got quite dizzy. I tried to ride again, but got lightheaded again. As I was leaning over my handlebars, a guy in a pickup truck stopped. He was an ex-military guy who said, "Man, you are almost at the point of heat exhaustion." I could hardly stand up.

He had no water in his truck, so he waved down another vehicle. It happened to be a family with two children, and they had water. They put me into their SUV with the air conditioning to rest and cool off.

After about 30 minutes, I saw them put my bike into the back of the pickup truck, and the military guy took me to Umatilla, where I was going to end my day's ride. It wasn't more than 10 to 20 miles, but it didn't matter at that point. I just knew that if I tried to continue on my own in the condition that I was in, I would not have made it. Who knows what condition I would have been in? I could only imagine that I would have fainted, fallen off my bike, and just laid on the ground in the heat. What a blessing that this man came along when he did! Again, this is another sign that God was watching over me.

My sister Lois had called the local fire department about my situation, and the Fire Chief on duty not only got us a room, but he paid for it.

That night, I met up with my friend Tom Reinhardt, who drove from Seattle, Washington, to meet me in Umatilla. We had a great evening, and the next day, I was ready to go again.

Tom gave me his helmet, which had a light mounted on top that was both a spotlight and a strobe light. All I can say is - it sure came in handy and was just another Blessing. I won't forget that day and decided that I would only take an energy drink in the morning before I started the ride and at noon when I stopped for lunch. I would never mix it in my water containers again.

> **Thoughts for the Day:** The sun can certainly take its toll on your body, and again, I wasn't consuming enough water. Why, you may ask? There was no place to stop and get more. My throat was sore from the dryness, and I was really starting to feel the effects of dehydration. How can I fix this?

Day 6

Sunday, July 29; Umatilla, OR to Walla Walla, WA; Daily Miles 55; Total Miles 386.

Up again nice and early but decided to have a nice breakfast with my friend, Tom Reinhardt. I also met the fire chief, who was so gracious as to cover the cost of our motel room. He said that he and his local volunteer firefighters could appreciate the dedication my son and father had as firefighters, and the gesture was just a way to wish us much success and say, 'Keep going and stay safe.' Wow! What a feeling and tribute to all firefighters - THANK YOU!

We stayed on the Oregon side of the Colorado River on Highway 730. It was not a difficult ride but offered a number of scenic lookout spots overlooking the Colorado River and mountains. Absolutely beautiful country but rugged in its beauty. I took a picture of the state line sign: "Welcome to Washington, the Evergreen State," and it sure was. Gorgeous country, but the lack of places to ride along the road was challenging.

There were large expanses of open land, as well as fields of growing wheat, I think. The combines were huge. Dozens of them were harvesting in what appeared as just one field. Hot open country, and again, water was an issue. I stopped whenever I could get it.

The state is rich in history depicting Lewis and Clark, fur traders, the use of steamboats on the river, the railroad, and the native Indians. I stopped every chance I got to rest, but also to read through the numerous historical accounts along the way.

Ride for Jakob 67

> **Thoughts for the Day:** I was curious about how I would feel today. I woke up feeling good: no dizzy spells, no soreness, and the only mental feeling I had was a sense of pride for having come this far already. I don't think it would have been possible without the Mannatech supplements. This journey is definitely a learning experience in endurance and listening to my body.

DAY 7

Monday, July 30; Walla Walla, WA to Pomeroy, WA; Daily Miles 65; Total Miles 451 and 8 hours of riding.

Walla Walla was a nice city to ride through, and as we left at 8:30 a.m., it became obvious it was going to be another hot one. The temperature just did not want to cooperate and the temperatures got to the high 90's. The area was dry and dusty along the highway due to the number of fields being combined. There was very little breeze, so the dust hung in the air.

As I got to Waitsburg, you could see combines in almost every field. An interesting sight was small twister-type funnels going across the fields, and you could see little dust tornadoes, as I called them. I never experienced any of them, but I sure thought it might be nice to ride through one just to cool off. That never happened.

I ran out of water AGAIN! It was so hard to judge just how much water to carry. Any extra weight over and above what I was already carrying was, at times, just too much, and I had no way at that point to get rid of the extra baggage. So, running out of water was something I just had to contend with.

As I was riding along the highway, I could see small farmhouses or homesteads tucked into the cluster of trees where there obviously was water. These small homesteads were something to see. I was seeing firsthand a part of America that I never thought I would ever see or experience.

Finally, I came across this farm that wasn't too far off the highway. I had to get water, so I rode into the yard. The farmer was standing next to his combine, and I surprised him as he didn't hear me coming on my bike. He sure didn't expect a bike rider to stop by. He said, "Man, what are you doing out here and in this heat?"

Yeah, I wondered that myself. Anyway, I explained that I needed water. What was so incredible was that he took me to his pump, and I could not believe how COLD the water was. I not only filled up every container I had, but I also took the hose and covered myself completely. It didn't matter if I looked like I peed my shorts; it just felt GOOD!!!

Now, this is interesting. I knew my sister had been following me on my travels and called the local Police and Fire Departments to keep an eye out for me. As I was approaching Dayton, the Colombia County Sheriff passed me and kept going. Little did I know he was looking for me and had turned around. He passed me again and pulled over. He got out of the car, and as he approached, I said, "I know, I know you got me for speeding. What can I say?"

We had a good laugh, and we talked about my ride for Jakob. He told me, 'Be careful in this heat, especially at your age.' Then he added, "At any age, actually, with the heat we are experiencing this year." He expressed how impressed he was with what I was doing. It sure felt good when people you don't know give you a compliment. You just never know how your actions impact others.

I found I never really felt concerned about my safety from others wishing me harm at any time during the journey. People everywhere were so helpful and considerate. They honked their horns as they drove by waving, stopped to wish me a safe journey, and donated to Jakob's Ride all along the way. WOW! Another blessing.

The only thing I had to contend with when riding on the shoulder of the road was broken glass, rubber, and steel fibers from blown tires, wood debris, and dead snakes, most of which were dead rattlesnakes that had been hit on the roads at night. I never touched one, believe me.

> **Thoughts for the Day:** I've been on this ride now for a week and I'm feeling good. I'm pacing myself, stopping when needed, drinking water regularly, and taking Empact+ when I stop for lunch. This stuff is good!

Day 8

Tuesday, July 31; Pomeroy, WA, to Lewiston, ID; Daily Miles 35; Total Miles 486. We left at 9:30 a.m. Today was going to be a short day. Now entering our 3rd state.

It was only 100 today. One long hill to climb, but the downhill was awesome - 12 miles long. I had to break all the way. There were times I reached 30 mph plus - too fast for me. My hands hurt just braking constantly. It's interesting going that fast and having semis passing you. All I could do was hang on.

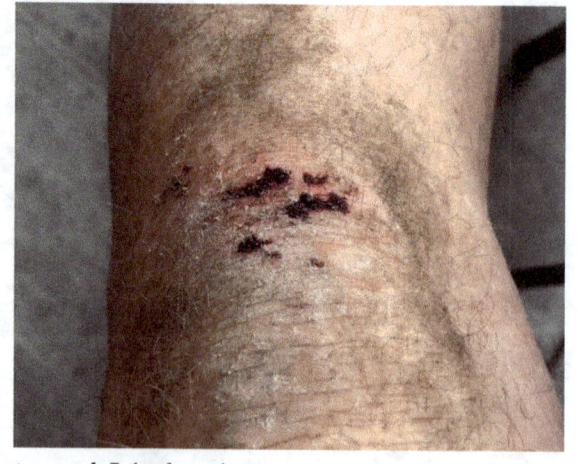

Later in the day, I had another spill and cut my leg again. Same knee, more blood. Thank goodness I was wearing a helmet. My bike needed servicing again, and I had to buy a new seat. Something a little softer, if you know what I mean.

The road we are taking tomorrow will have a lot of construction. It's going to be interesting.

Seeing each state slide behind us excites me, even more so when I consider what this ride means for Jakob. Several people have just walked up to me and donated - WOW! Another blessing for Jakob. I hope every person knows that by supporting this RIDE, you touched his life!

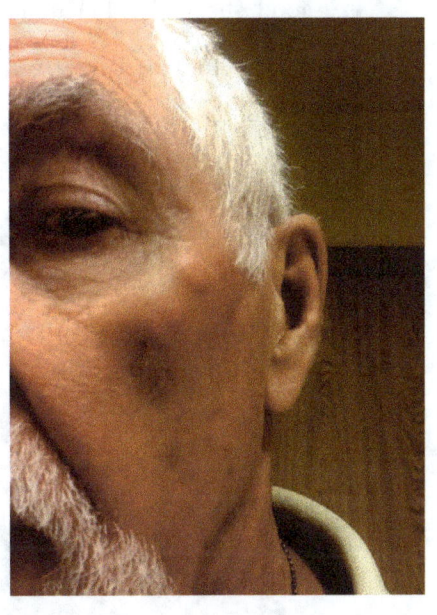

As we rode into Lewiston, we were met by the local Fire & Police Chiefs. Again, my sister had made contact with these men, giving me a greater sense of security. They told us that from time to time, they would follow our route just to see that all was well, and they did. They also gave me their cell numbers in case I needed help because they knew how heavy the traffic was at this time of the year.

As I have said so many times before, it was a relief to know that people were watching out for us as we moved forward. What a great feeling!

Thoughts for the Day: At one point today, I sat on the side of the road thinking about what is happening physically. Here I am, a 70-year-old man, and in good shape, BUT I don't FEEL like I'm 70 (or at least what I think a 70-year-old riding across the country should feel like). Hmm? What is different with me? Could these supplements really be making that much of a difference?

Day 9

Wednesday, August 1; Lewiston, ID to Orofino, ID; Daily Miles 35; Total Miles 521. We left Lewiston at 8:30 a.m. The temperature was in the high 80's but reached over 100 again. Today's ride was actually very scary/hairy.

Throughout the ride, there were lots of big trucks, and since this was vacation time, there were also a lot of cars/trucks pulling trailers, so it was very busy. I stopped at a rest area and was going to walk down to the Clearwater River. I met a guy from the Fish & Wildlife branch who suggested that I not do that. I asked why, and he said, "Lots of poison ivy and rattlesnakes." So, I passed.

About 3 miles from Orofina, the local Police Chief was made aware of our ride and purpose by my sister Lois. He asked if he could give us an escorted ride into town. Heck yeah! One vehicle in front with lights flashing, then Jim and I, and one police car following us with flashers going. I am sure people were wondering what was going on. So, we were celebrities for a moment. The chief also got us a room at the best hotel in the city, and the owner said - no charge - WOW! Blessings, blessings, blessings.

To top it all off, a man stopped me and asked, "So, who is Jakob?" I told him the story, and he donated $100. He said he has a son who, in his youth, had somewhat similar conditions, so he knows how I feel and what the family must face daily. He said to me - keep going, brother - be safe. WOW again.

Today, I was also interviewed by a local newspaper journalist who was writing a story about the RIDE FOR JAKOB. She asked about the products I was taking, and she said she knew the value of good nutrition. Also, the chief is posting Jakob's Facebook link and attaching it to theirs. God is so good!

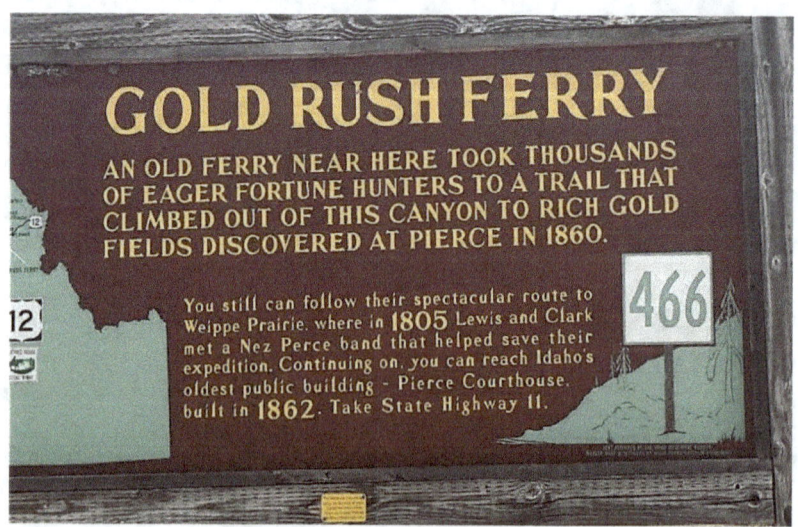

Day 10

Thursday, August 2; Orofino, ID to Lowell, ID; Daily Miles 57; Total Miles 578. Temperatures over 102 again.

We left Orofino at 9:30 a.m. Our destination is Lowell, Idaho. One main concern today is the condition of Highway 12. The road through the mountains was never straight, making it difficult to judge traffic conditions. Several times during the day, semis and campers forced me to stop, get off my bike, and let them pass.

Three police cars passed me with sirens going. Turned out there was a serious accident ahead. The road was closed for over 1 ½ hours. We saw both vehicles that hit head-on, and we heard that one person died and the second (not sure) died shortly thereafter. We still had 30 miles to go.

This was not a good day to ride or travel on this type of highway. The scenery was incredible. This would be a great place to vacation, with great fishing, white water rafting, and sightseeing. Lowell has a population of 23. We found a place for the night, Three Rivers Campground, and got the last room. Tomorrow will be another long day of over 80 miles, as there is no place to stop, no stores to buy water, and today we had NO cell service or connections.

Therefore, I couldn't post any messages about the day's travel and events on Facebook. As it turned out, we would not have any cell service for at least the next 2 days. The problem was that I could not call my riding partner for any help or assistance, nor anyone else, for that matter. He was many miles ahead of me at all times. I realized I had no connection to the outside world other than the people driving by who might help me if I needed it.

DAY 11

Friday, August 3; Lowell, ID to Lolo Pass, MT; Daily Miles 86; Total Miles 664. We left Lowell at 9 a.m. Had a good breakfast and hit the road. After what we experienced yesterday and talking with locals, I knew the highway was going to get worse and narrower. The ride today was still hot.

Some areas were somewhat dark as we were riding through a very dense forest area. I made sure I put on my strobe lights on the back of my bike and on my helmet just to be seen. We encountered major construction that held up traffic. They would not let us pass on our bikes, and in the first construction area, they loaded our bikes on a pilot vehicle and carried us through the 2 miles closed down.

There was an accident the day before, where a very large flatbed semi carrying a large building crane couldn't make the turn, and it slid off the highway, going into the river. It got hung up on the rocks, and the cab of the truck was still on the main part of the road. They were waiting for a special crane to come to see if it could be pulled out of the river.

We came across another construction zone, and this time, a couple in a large motor home loaded our bikes and took us through the area and to the next pull-out about 5 miles. Another nice break in the day. They offered to take us all the way to Lolo Hot Springs, and as much as I wanted to, we declined the offer and made the ride.

With each turn in the road and the narrow conditions, I wished I had taken them up on their offer. Oh well. At times, it was more difficult going downhill than going up due to the wind conditions. What made the ride more dangerous is that, in most areas, it dropped off dramatically to the river below.

I almost had a serious accident. I was riding along a guard rail and following the white line that had no more than a foot to ride on. I heard one of the large semis coming behind me, but I couldn't see him because I had broken my mirror on an earlier fall. I unclipped my right foot and put my leg down to stop, but I couldn't get my left foot unclipped fast enough. The wind from the semi pulled me into the traffic, and I swerved out to get my balance in front of a pickup right behind him. That was a close one.

A person stopped me to say, "Be careful; the next 20 miles are going to be similar." He offered to take me through that specific area just to be safe. I took him up on the offer, and I am sure glad I did. The climb to the top of the Lolo Pass was very long and high. Lolo Pass is where the time change took place on our route.

My friend Dennis Blackburn told us he would meet us at the Lola Pass Visitors Center, and we would spend the night there before going on to Missoula, Montana, the next day. Dennis brought food, and we had a nice camp meal. Watching his dog chase the local prairie dogs down their hole was fun, but he never caught one.

Dennis and his dog slept in the back of his pickup truck. For us, he laid out a rolled-up mattress with a blanket that we could lie on and cover up with. Well, the temperature got down to 33 degrees that night, and it was cold, to say the least. Fortunately, I still had most of my clothes and heavy gear, so I took advantage of them.

On the other hand, Jim did not have extra clothes to wear and had to sleep in his riding clothes. I woke in the middle of the night to go to the restroom, and  you'll never guess what I saw: Jim was sitting under the hand dryer, pushing the button constantly to get warm. It really was a funny sight. Even with the cold, I enjoyed the clear night sky and the stars.

The mountain rivers flowing beside the highway as they  meandered through the mountains were an awesome sight to see. Crystal clear waters, and from time to time, I stopped and watched a man fly fishing in the middle of the river. Now that's fishing. Just watching the fly being lifted with the fly rod and landing on the water. It really was a sight to see. What beauty!

Day 12

Saturday, August 4; Lolo Pass, MT to Missoula, MT; Daily Miles 43; Total Miles 707. We made it to the Montana state line.

We got up early, but I admit I didn't sleep well. It was a cold, clear night under the stars, so peaceful, but not conducive to quality sleep.

Dennis, Jim, and I enjoyed a great tour of the Visitors Center, which is a great piece of history about Lewis & Clark, the struggles they encountered getting through  this area, and the issues they experienced with the Indians they encountered.

 It was apparent what traveling must have been like in their time, with the mountains, steep wooded valleys, and no trails to follow. Just riding along the highway alone was enough to help me visualize and experience a small part of what they must have

gone through. Knowing what I faced on this route, I could only imagine their struggles.

After the tour, we continued to Missoula, Montana, where Dennis graciously offered to open his home to us for the weekend. He cooked a wonderful meal and offered to let us relax in his hot tub. That was an incredible evening to remember and a great rest. Thank you, Dennis!

Day 13

Sunday, August 5.

We decided to take another day off and relax. Dennis asked if we wanted to go tubing down the local river. A lot of people were out enjoying the day, as it was again very hot. Drifting along the river and enjoying the scenery was so pleasant and definitely a different pace.

I went through my gear and decided to downsize to lighten the load. Dennis shipped all my extra clothes and nonessentials to my wife in Grand Rapids. I can't believe I traveled all those miles with so much. What a relief it was to have less baggage. If anyone asked me

Ride for Jakob 85

what my top advice would be for a long-distance ride, I would definitely recommend making your pannier bags as light as you can!

Dennis gave me some freeze-dried food to cook if I needed to stop and camp. He used to do white water rafting rides down the Grand Canyon and took this kind of food to cook for his group. I thought this was awesome and couldn't thank him enough.

That being said, I went out and bought a camp-type stove that you could put in your backpack to cook this type of meal. I also picked up a 2-man tent. Now, I am ready for the unexpected. Thanks again, Dennis!

Previously, I had asked Jan to send the next shipment of Mannatech nutritional supplements that I would need to Dennis' house. I knew I'd be seeing him at some point, so this allowed me to carry less to start with. I also packed these up and felt good about getting rid of all the extra baggage.

DAY 14

Monday, August 6; Missoula, MT to Lincoln, MT; Daily Miles 73; Total Miles 780.

We left Missoula at 11:30 a.m., later than normal. We went to the Adventure Cycling offices to upgrade Jim's GPS for traveling east.

Thirteen miles out of Missoula, with no cell service, Jim got flat #5. Just after fixing it, another flat plus his tire ripped open. As I mentioned throughout this ride, the heat was unbearable at times. I flagged down a fish & wildlife truck, and he took Jim back to Missoula to get another tire and more inner tubes.

I kept going and met a woman cyclist who was stopped along the highway, taking a break, but going in my direction. We rode together for 25 miles. She was a San Francisco teacher taking a two-week biking vacation through the mountains.

At the only gas station along the route, some 40 miles from Missoula, Jim finally caught up to me. We met another guy from Spain who was mountain biking. We all visited for a while, and then went our separate ways. Meeting cyclists from so many parts of the

US and other countries along the route was definitely a highlight of the journey.

About 2 miles down the road, I discovered I had left my CamelBak on the bench at the gas station. This water pack goes over your shoulder so you can drink more easily. Bummer! So, I had to go back. Every mile is important, but now that I had to go back, it bugged me. Anyway, I got about ¼ mile from the station,  and a motorcycle biker came along and handed me my CamelBak. You meet so many wonderful people!

The biggest issue on this part of the ride was that there was nowhere to ride safely. The roads through the mountains were just too narrow and scary. Yet, I was surprised at the number of cyclists using the Louis & Clark trail. I arrived in Lincoln at 9:30 p.m. after sunset. Too long a day, and it was HOT! I had a shower, ate at a local bar and grill, and went to bed. I got a severe neck cramp and had it all day. How I got it, I don't know, but it sure made it difficult to ride.

Today, I had a very long downhill ride or run. I don't recall just how long the downhill run was, but it went for several miles. It was a relief not having to push uphill continually, but the downhill run can be just as challenging.

Again, I had to apply the brakes constantly. My hands started to cramp up and were difficult to open. It felt nice to drift down the long grade, but it sure added some additional issues to contend with. The crosswinds occasionally hit you when you were not expecting them. It made you wonder, if you fell off your bike going this fast, what would happen to you and your bike? That being said, I just kept my hands on the brakes, front and back, at all times. I knew I had to adjust my cables as soon as possible, which turned out to be longer than expected.

Thoughts for the Day: Two weeks in – I'm feeling good! Now that I've worked out the hydration issues and the Mannatech supplements have really kicked in, I am truly impressed!

Day 15

Tuesday, August 7; Lincoln, MT to Great Falls, MT; Daily Miles 97; Total Miles 877. Now over 800 miles.

We left Lincoln at 9:30 a.m., knowing today would be a long one. There were no places to stop to eat or get water, so Cliff Bars, Empact+, and water had to be stretched out. My bike fell over after I parked it next to a road sign and bent my fender guard, which rubbed my tire. I straightened it out and kept going.

Finally, the mountains are behind us—hooray. It was a memorable ride through some of the most beautiful country I have ever seen. I don't think I will do this ride again, but it is a great place to vacation, and I recommend it to anyone.

Tonight, we were blessed again. A couple with an RV we met in the Lolo Pass area gave us a ride through a construction zone. They gave us their address and telephone number and said that if we decided to come through Great Falls, we could stay with them for the night. I called them, and they not only gave us a place to sleep in their RV but fed us a wonderful meal as well.

They have a daughter named Leahia. She was born with a health condition that made her unable to walk or talk. They were able to get her a device that enabled her to communicate with them and live a life that touches everyone.

It just reminded me so much of Jakob and what his world must be like. I often wonder what Jakob thinks. What does he understand? What would he like to say? There must be so much in his mind that he wants to express and say. I know that when I come to visit, he

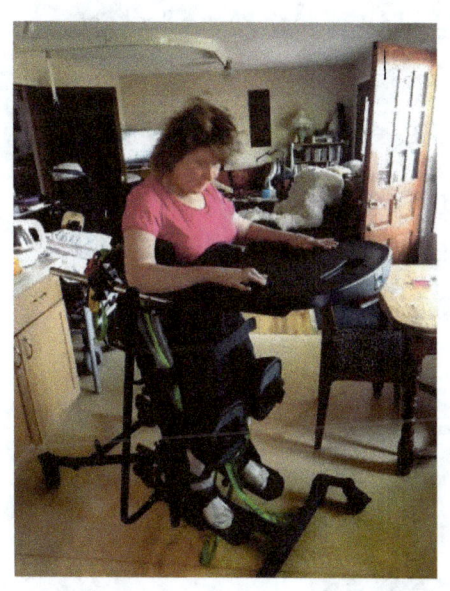

immediately has a smile of recognition on his face and he always wants to take me 'somewhere.' Living in a body that won't allow you to say what you want has to be so frustrating.

The couple we stayed with told me that when Leahia started communicating with the program, they discovered that the world opened up not only to her but also to her parents. They said she had so many things she wanted to say but just did not know how to say them.

This inspired me. I was going to do whatever it took to make this ride a success for Jakob. What I saw in this young woman was so inspiring. Thank you, LEAHIA, for who you are and what you have done to encourage me and so many others. Again, we met some wonderful people along this ride!

Now, heading east, finally going through Montana and the prairies. This has been an AWESOME ADVENTURE, one I will never forget. So far, no major health issues other than a stiff neck.

> **Thoughts for the Day:** I don't know why I got a stiff neck; maybe it's because I was sleeping so well, or maybe it's from holding it at the same angle while riding for hours. It wasn't serious, just annoying. I suspect water intake, meaning not drinking enough, was a factor as well. Thankfully, the kink was short-lived and didn't affect the ride.

DAY 16

Wednesday, August 8; Great Falls, MT to Lewistown, MT; Daily Miles 105; Total Miles 982. It was my longest ride and distance to date, and it was a tough one: hot, rolling, long hills to climb.

We left Great Falls at 8:30 a.m., knowing today was going to be a very long day, but we didn't realize just how long. It was HOT again. Tomorrow, they are giving a hot weather warning. The heat takes a lot out of you—one stretch of 45 miles and nowhere to get water. Dehydration is a big issue, and water is heavy to carry. Towns are too far apart for anything. I stopped a lot just to rest.

The area I was riding in seemed like a high plains area with lots of rolling hills. It was a road with no traffic at all. A lady came by in a pickup truck, pulled over beside me, and said, 'What are you doing way out here, especially in this heat?'

I explained the purpose of my ride and that this was the road suggested on my map. She said that she didn't have a lot of water as she was just going to let her cattle out for grazing down the road. Knowing how hot it was, though, she said, "Come in and sit here for a few minutes to cool off with the air conditioner going."

Now, you would wonder why she would ever suggest that I get into the truck with her all alone, especially in this part of the country. Well, let me tell you. In the back seat (it was a crew cab pickup), she had a large German Shepherd that I did not see until I got in the front seat. He sat up, and it was obvious he was her personal guard dog. I could feel his breath on my shoulder as his nose was inches from my neck. All I could think of was 'nice doggy.' She assured me that I did not have to be concerned, but I can tell you I felt great relief when I got out of the truck. She wished me much success and told me that just down the road, a few miles, I would find a fuel service station. I needed water badly and stopped at this station.

The guy who was there delivered fuel to the area ranchers. His water was so cold! When I told him what I was doing, he said, "Are you a believer?" I answered in the affirmative. So, he prayed for me and told me the road ahead was not friendly to cyclists. He was right. We planned to stop at a motel in Stanford, but it was closed, and the owner was nowhere to be found. After making several attempts to reach him with the number we had, we decided to keep going to Lewiston. This was too far for one day's ride. 60 is tops for me!

I had a flat tire! I knew it was going to happen to me at some point. Guess where it happened, though? It went flat as I leaned my bike against the wall of our motel room. The Interstate was over 2 miles from the town and the motel. I picked up this steel belt fragment on the highway but could still travel that distance to the motel before my tire went flat. Another blessing - God is so AWESOME!

I had not changed a tire on this bike yet, and I was sure glad Jim was there for guidance. Breaking down in the middle of nowhere was something I really dreaded.

I think we have three more days of riding in Montana, at least. I am not looking forward to the road ahead.

Day 17

Thursday, August 9; Lewistown, MT to Winnett, MT; Daily Miles 52; Total Miles 1034. Over the 1000 mark and just 2500 to go!

We left Lewistown at 9:30 a.m. I can't believe I've been on my bike for over 1000 miles! The road conditions were not as bad as I was told they would be. It was long, flat country with a few rolling hills, no shade, and no service to get a rest break or water.

My water HAD to last for the entire day, and all I can carry is 1½ gallons for weight. Adding weight makes the ride more difficult. I am still carrying too

much weight for a trip like this. When I get to Grand Rapids, I will restructure my bags and needs list to lighten the load dramatically. It makes it difficult to control the front wheel for steering sometimes.

The only thing exciting that happened today is that two large Mule deer ran across the road right in front of me. I had a deer hit the side of my van not too long ago, but I wasn't prepared to be run over by a deer on my bike! It was close, though. The traffic was sparse, so I took advantage of the road, so cars and trucks had to go around me. At the end of the day, 7 hours in 104 degrees of heat for 52 miles just wore me out. We got to our motel, and I stayed in a COLD shower for over 20 minutes. I had dinner and crashed. Getting ready for tomorrow's ride of over 70 miles in this heat again.

FORT MAGINNIS

Established in 1880, Fort Maginnis was located about 8 miles north of here. This country was great buffalo range before that time, but cattlemen were bringing in stock from the western valleys and cowboys trailed Texas longhorns in from the southeast. There wasn't room for both cattle and buffalo, so the latter had to go. Soldiers protected cattle from being mistaken for buffalo by hungry Indians, encouraged settlement of the Judith Basin west of here and patrolled the Carroll Road to keep supplies rolling between Carroll (near the mouth of the Musselshell River) and Helena. By 1890 the post was no longer needed, the threatening Indians having been relegated to reservations, and the fort was abandoned with civilian blessings.

There were also quite a number of palefaced parties who were handy with a branding iron and prone to make errors as to ownership of their neighbors' cattle. Such careless souls were known as 'rustlers.' Sometimes the cattlemen called on these pariahs with a posse and intimated that they were unpopular with a hangman's noose. Usually such a visitation cured a rustler or two permanently.

Just an added note. There were many signs along this area. Apparently, it was once known for massive buffalo herds, but things changed dramatically when the settlers moved into the Montana area with cattle. It said there wasn't room for both cattle and buffalo, so the buffalo had to go. Soldiers came in and literally wiped out the buffalo herds. I read a lot of interesting history about the West and its changes as it was being explored and settled.

BEARPAW SHALE AND THE INLAND OCEAN

The black shale rocks seen in this area represent the muddy sediments deposited by the last ocean to exist in Montana. The shale, known by geologists as the Bearpaw Shale contains fossils of sea-going creatures that lived and died some 70 million years ago. Twenty foot long swimming reptiles like Mosasaurus and Tylosaurus fed on fishes and ammonites, relatives of squids and octopi. The remains of the gigantic coiled ammonites called Placentaceras and the straight shelled ammonites called Baculites are often found in these shale deposits. This inland ocean extended north to south, from the Gulf of Mexico to the Arctic Ocean, and divided North America into two subcontinents. Dinosaurs roamed the lands, and alligators and turtles inhabited the streams and rivers. But, one of the largest animals to live in this area was a gigantic, forty foot long crocodile called Deinosuchus that lived in the coastal waters of the inland seaway. The first remains of this animal were found near here. In the early 1900s, geologists learned that geological structures called anticlines, a kind of large wrinkle in the rock strata, were good places to drill for oil. Geologists also realized that certain parts of anticlines were better than others, and that the good spots were beneath structures they called domes. Here at the Mosby rest area you are standing on a part of the Mosby Dome, of the Cat Creek Anticline.

Day 18

Friday, August 10; Winnett, MT to Jordon, MT; Daily Miles 75; Total Miles 1109.

We left Winnett at 9:30 a.m. It was HOT again. Today's temperature was 105, and there was no wind to cool you off. The only somewhat cool air was what I experienced going downhill. Flat country with *long* rolling hills. Going uphill in this heat just knocks you out. At 20 miles out was a rest area with COLD water, then another 20 miles, another rest area - water again. Last 35 miles - nothing - tough ride and slow going.

Again, I realized that I need to really be selective on what to carry, as everything weighs something, and it just adds up. I wanted to get rid of stuff, but I can't until I get to Grand Rapids. The last leg will be very different. Overall, I am enjoying the ride and seeing lots of the country. It's funny, but cows look at you as you ride by. I think they are thinking - this guy is crazy! At least we had a shade tree today.

I wish I could add all my pictures of the scenery and landscape. It is hard to put into words just how flat and yet rolling this country is and what is grown in this part of America.

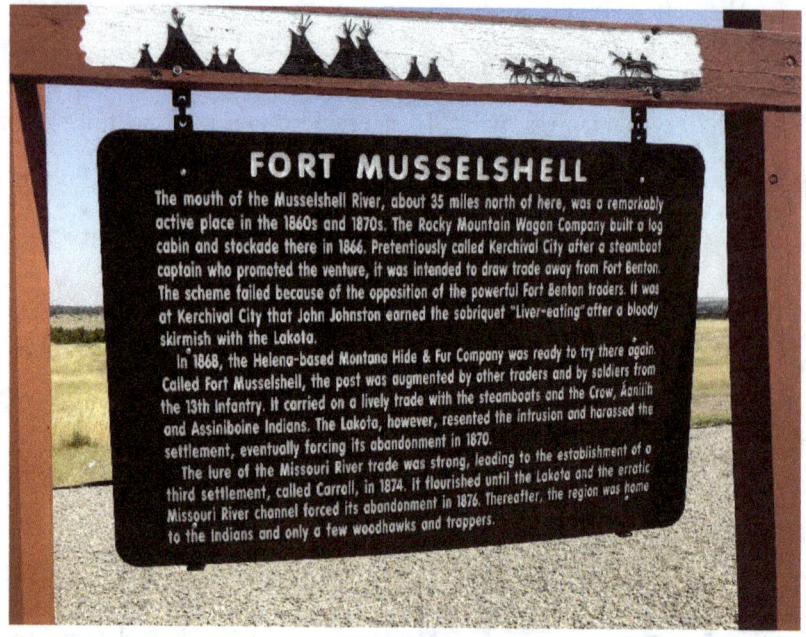

DAY 19

Saturday, August 11; Jordon, MT to Circle, MT; Daily Miles 67; Total Miles 1176.

We left Jordon at 8:30 a.m. It was cooler this morning, but the temperature rose quickly to 105, and it stayed there all day. Flat country, but the roads were narrow, so we were forced to ride on the main part of the highway. Actually, that was a good thing because where there was a wider shoulder the debris was excessive. Jim had two more flat tires from the steel-belted tire fragments that littered the sides of the roads.

Traffic was light. It was tough going up hills, but the ride downhill was nice. Again, the only breeze you could get - just long miles of nothing. The first watering hole or rest stop was Flowing Wells. Cold water – nice! We were 35 miles out of Jordan and had another 30 miles to go. The heat takes the energy out of you - many stops to rest.

I met a couple along the route and got water from them. Man, did I need it. The problem with Montana is the distance between any kind of town or place to get water or to find shade and get out of the sun. I hear North Dakota is the same. I can't wait to get to Minnesota - I think! Only because the towns, cities, and rest stops are closer together.

I met a guy cyclist who is riding his bike around the world. He started in the

UK, traveled across Europe, Turkey, China, and now the U.S. He has been on his ride now for 14 months. Cool guy. I had dinner with him. He's camping all the way.

Another guy cyclist from the U.S. is also riding his bike across America and staying at the same motel. It looks like we are all traveling east tomorrow. You meet great people from all over the world.

DAY 20

Sunday, August 12; Circle, MT to Glendive, MT; Daily Miles 45; Total Miles 1221.

We left Circle, MT at 9:30 a.m. The temperature was pleasant when we started, but again, it soon climbed to 105 plus. Everyone we talked to made some kind of comment about the heat, especially this year.

At the beginning of the day, there were long hills to climb and some over 2 miles going up. The first 25 miles had very few downhill runs once you got to the top, and then you saw another long ride ahead of you with another long hill to climb. Tough to ride at times. Most times, I got off my bike and just walked, not necessarily due to the long uphill ride, but simply because of the heat. I had to wear my leg coverings designed with UV protection and another around my neck. When I got a chance, I poured cold water over them just to cool off.

The ride today was somewhat boring, and nothing really to take pictures of; even the traffic was sparse. The last 20 miles of the 45-mile ride to get to Glendive was FLAT. No hills at all, and HOT! I went through most of the 2 gallons of water I was carrying.

The route showed a stop called Lindsay. All stores were closed when I arrived, and most had gone out of business. That being said, I had to make sure my water lasted.

Apparently, this is dinosaur country, and the local museum has a

large display of discovered bones. However, it was closed today, being Sunday, and again tomorrow, so I was not able to get pictures.

Glendive is our last town/stop in Montana, and tomorrow, we start the ride across North Dakota. My bike is running smoothly, but it does need a few adjustments. Our next city is Medora, ND. Apparently, there is a cycle shop to get things looked after. The suggested miles are approximately 61. I was blessed today when two people gave me $10 after seeing my sign: RIDE FOR JAKOB.

DAY 21

Monday, August 13; Glendive, MT to Medora, ND; Daily Miles 65; Total Miles 1286. I am now in North Dakota. Four states down and nine to go.

We left Glendive, MT, at 8 a.m. The weather was much cooler but still sunny. It only got into the 90s, and I am now calling this COOLER! I think my brain has been fried.

We traveled on and off the interstate. It has a broad paved shoulder but is full of debris. Our worst issue is picking up steel fragments from blown steel-belted tires. So far, I have had only one flat tire. Tomorrow is all interstate. Most of the day, the wind was a 'crosswind,' which made it difficult to

keep a straight ride, with lots of wavering from side to side. On a back road for some 27 miles, I encountered NO traffic at all. You would think I was in NO man's Land. On one long hill, I got a strong tailwind that literally pushed me uphill. Now, is that cool - it never happened again.

Here's one for you. I was on another back road because we couldn't ride on the interstate. This was a 35-mile ride. For over 2½ hours, no one passed me, and Jim was already miles ahead of me. So, I was again by myself. I came around a turn, and there, standing broadside in the middle of the road, was a range bull and three cows in the ditch. So, what do I do - after all, it's just a cow! - I approach it slowly.

I got to about 20 yards from him, and he turned to face me; his head dropped, but didn't move. So, I got off my bike because if he decided to charge me, all I could think was, "My bike! If it got damaged, then what would I do?"

If there ever was a time for help, it was now, so I yelled, "GOD, I need you now!" Now, here's the amazing thing. Like I said before, I'd had hours of no traffic. Right at that moment, a car approached me from behind. I didn't even see or hear it coming. The car slowly passed me, approached the bull, and the bull moved off the road and into the ditch! I thought, "If I don't go now, this may be my only opening," so I got on my bike and rode past him as fast as I could. Now ponder this: the car just kept on going, and I didn't see another vehicle on that road from that moment on. There is no other explanation for this one car, so I know Someone was looking after me!

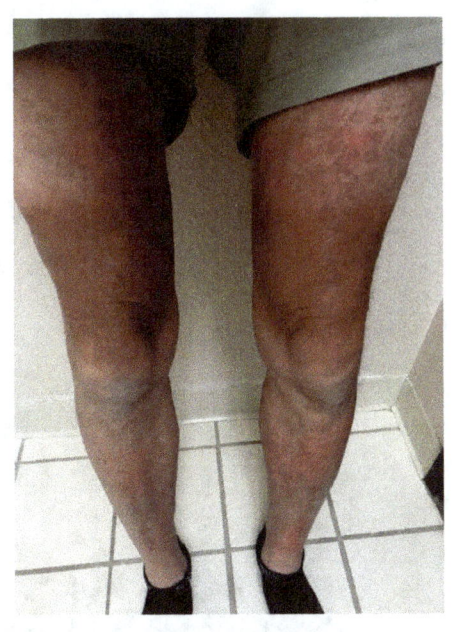

There was only one other issue that day. I got severe heat rash on my legs from the sun and heat. It didn't hurt or burn, but this had never happened before, even on those 105-degree days. I have been

putting sunscreen on every day, and I'm sure it will go away in a few days. Again, I have no muscle pain, cramps, or any kind of fatigue or joint pain other than the cramp in my neck. I think the neck cramp has to be from leaning forward on my bike for so long each day. I think my neck is just getting tired.

Medora is a neat town. There is a lot of history about Teddy Roosevelt, who spent some time there, and lots of American history, too. I got a picture standing by Teddy Roosevelt. (Or at least a statue of him!)

I also ran into the guy I met in Circle, who was riding his bike around the world, at the bike shop where he was getting his bike serviced as well. That was a nice surprise. He sure had some awesome stories to share. I sure would like to do that sometime in the future. Hey, who knows?

Ride for Jakob

Also, a lady approached me at the motel where we were staying. She was on vacation with her three children and was excited about my ride and wanted to know more about Jakob. She said she wanted to share this with her children.

Day 22

Tuesday, August 14; Medora, ND to Hebron, ND; Daily Miles 77; Total Miles 1363. It was a long day. We are now in the central time zone. Tomorrow heading for Bismarck, ND.

We left Medora at 8:30 a.m. Part of the ride was on I-94, but mostly on Old Highway 10, which ran parallel to the interstate. I preferred #10 because there is no debris on the road. Since the traffic was next to nothing or very light for the most part, I really had the entire road to myself.

This was an uneventful day compared to yesterday. The temperature was cooler, and there was mild wind, but it was still quite sunny. There were long hills to climb again, and it will likely be like that

throughout North Dakota.

In Dickerson, I stopped to eat lunch. On my way out of town, a truck pulled up beside me, and the woman said: I read about you and Jakob, here's $40 - WOW! I am not sure what the article said and just where it came from or who sent it out. I do know I did an interview in Portland and Orofino. But how awesome is that! People donating that I don't even know.

One interesting thing that I saw was many bee hive boxes where people had a business collecting honey. Also, there were fields upon fields of sunflowers. I once saw a picture painted that was titled "A Field of Sunflowers," but when you actually see acres of sunflowers, it is absolutely a beautiful sight. Now I know where they get sunflower seeds from. DUH!

There was a time in the day when it was again very hot. I was riding in another area with many winding roads, and the terrain was constantly forcing me to ride up long hills and short down runs. The heat sure causes you to fatigue quickly. I got to a point at almost high noon when I was starting to feel a little lightheaded AGAIN! I knew that if I didn't take it slow, I could have the same issue with getting overheated as I did before. Especially since I was once AGAIN riding alone and with no cell service.

You won't believe what happened next…

I was praying and talking out loud to God. "GOD, please give me a sign that you are with me." As I turned the next curve, I looked up at the mountain right in front of me, and on the very top was a CROSS! I couldn't stop staring at it.

I realize the photo might not LOOK authentic, or some might think I had it photoshopped in, but it was REAL! It still gives me goosebumps to understand that God heard me and is faithful. At that moment, I knew to the depth of my being He was telling me that all was going to be OK. In fact, the next several miles were very easy riding. Although there was very little traffic, and I rode virtually alone during that time, I had a great sense of peace.

> **Thoughts for the Day:** I found a large rock I could lean against where I could see that cross and took a short break in awe. The thought that kept repeating in my head was, "God is good."
>
> I am now three weeks into this ride. As I sat there, I realized that my physical condition at this point in the journey was nothing short of amazing. I kept my normal health routine, which typically left me with sore muscles for a few days after intense exertion. BUT, I wasn't having any of that normal soreness, and trust me, I was doing intense exertion!
>
> The only change I had made in my routine was taking the Mannatech nutritional supplements: Ambrotose Life, Empact+, and TruPlenish. I find this very interesting, and I'm asking myself, "Will this last?"

DAY 23

Wednesday, August 15; Hebron, ND to Bismarck, ND; Daily Miles 55; Total Miles 1418.

Left Hebron by 9:15 a.m. I got a call this morning from a couple of local TV stations in Bismarck and Fargo wanting to do an interview about my RIDE FOR JAKOB. What a blessing to be able to share Jakob's story and the purpose of my ride!

Yesterday evening I repacked my bags and downsized to just TWO! This would make my load much lighter. There was a post office next to the café where we were going to eat breakfast, so I was able to mail the extra bags home. I can't believe I traveled all this way with four bags!

On our way out of town, we passed this brick factory. Come to find out, they have been making bricks since 1904 and are the only brick factory in North Dakota! That is how Hebron got to be known as 'the brick city.' When you are riding a bike, you get a lot more time to take in the sights around you. Seeing all the bricks and people working around the factory was an interesting sight to see.

Up to this point in time, there were NO rail trails to ride on. A rail trail is a public path that has been built on an abandoned railroad route. They are usually well taken care of, off the main highways, and a popular biking route when available. I was looking forward to riding my first one to compare the experience with all the highway and interstate riding we'd done.

As I was riding along the Interstate the traffic started getting very heavy due to the vacation traffic and proximity to Bismark. I didn't mind riding on the Interstate (other than all the debris) because if I had any issues, there was always someone I could flag down who would be more than happy to help me.

Anyway, as I was coming into Bismarck, ND, the lady I met at the motel in Medora saw me and pulled over. She wanted to introduce me to her children and have me share my story with them. She offered to give me a ride to the Quality Inn a few miles away, and I really appreciated the help. The traffic and number of overpasses through that part of Bismarck would have made the ride more difficult. Plus, I was just plain tired.

When we got to the motel, I parked my bike by the front door. The flag I had declaring 'RIDE FOR JAKOB' was in front of a window. It just so happened that the window was that of the owner of the motel. He came out and asked a few questions about what I was doing. I explained why I was doing this ride, and he said, "Your room is covered for tonight."

Another blessing. I was so grateful to have a little extra rest today, as we had been going strong for several days in a row.

DAY 24

Thursday, August 16; Bismarck, ND to Jamestown, ND; Daily Miles 105; Total Miles 1523. A long day overall. We had a nice tailwind and some construction. After dinner, I went straight to sleep.

We left Bismarck at 8:30 a.m. for our destination of Medina, ND. Unfortunately, there were NO accommodations along I-94 and we would have had to go at least 6 miles north to the town. Not knowing what, if any, accommodations the town would offer, we decided to push on to Jamestown, ND - another 30 miles.

This was definitely prairie country. Lots of combines taking grain off of fields. I am not sure if it was wheat, oats, or what, but there sure were acres of open fields. Occasionally, there were what I'd call 'potholes' or small lakes. They were loaded with ducks. Being a duck hunter, I could sure see how a hunt in this area would be exciting. There were also statues of dinosaurs and posters telling travelers that this was an area where many bones and fossils had been found throughout this part of North Dakota.

DAY 25

Friday, August 17; Jamestown, ND to Fargo, ND; Daily Miles 94; Total Miles 1617. Today was a good day to ride: overcast, cool, and with a tailwind all the way to Fargo. Tomorrow, we will be in Minnesota - Yah!!!!!!

As I was leaving the Super 8 motel in Jamestown, two people came up to me and made a donation. One guy was from Canada.

We rode on I-94 and a frontage road most of the day. I encountered construction and was stopped for a few minutes. When talking to the guy, he asked about Jakob. He opened his wallet and said, "All I have left is $1, and it's yours."

He gave me his last dollar! How awesome is that! I had a nice talk with him, and he said, "Why don't you ride on the other lane that we just finished paving? There will be no traffic at all on that section." Wow, what a dream come true. For the next several miles, I had the entire  highway going east all to myself, and I took total advantage of it as I just swerved from lane to lane for miles and knew that this was MY ROAD!

I got to Valley City and a truck stop. A lady who passed me on I-94 approached me and asked about Jakob. I again told the story. She explained that she promotes special interest stories like this. She gave me her card and said she wanted to help me. She promised to put something together for all of her followers. I gave her my flyer for information. I have no idea what that developed into, but it was amazing to see. Two other guys at the truck stop saw Jakob's sign and donated as well. God is so good.

As I was riding along I-94, a pickup passed me and stopped a ways ahead of me. When I got to the truck, it was the owner of the

Quality Inn in Bismarck, Bernie! He just wanted to say 'hi' and wished me a successful and safe ride.

Then, I got a call from a local TV station in Fargo, ND, who wanted to do an interview when I got to Fargo. My sister, Lois, had made contact with them about my ride and purpose, and they wanted to do a story about my RIDE FOR JAKOB. We met that evening, and I had at least a 30-minute LIVE interview with Valley News Live. It aired the next day at 6 p.m.

They were impressed with what I was doing and wished me safe riding and much success. They said they would make sure this story gets out to the public.

As I was riding along the highway, I saw a billboard showing a picture of a Marine that said: Battles Are Won Within. At that time, it sure spoke to me because I have always believed that ALL BATTLES ARE WON WITHIN! It just gave me that internal boost to keep going and to make this ride the ride of a lifetime.

Day 26

Saturday, August 18; 5 states down and 6 to go. Today was a total day of rest in Fargo, ND. I needed it.

We were able to sleep in and just enjoy the day. We pushed hard for the past 10 days, going through Montana and North Dakota. Both of those states were the largest as far as distance travelled. Long rolling highways, but all travel was on the Interstate.

I rather liked this type of riding because it offered another layer of security if anything happened. Anyone would stop to help if needed. What I did not like was the shoulder to ride on. It was very wide, BUT every little bit, you had a broad band of rumble strips that you had to ride over, and they were pretty rough on a bike.

Also, in the rumble strips were fragments of glass, tire remains, and broken pieces of wood, not to mention the odd snake that was hit on the highway. Whenever possible, if there was no traffic going by me when I got to one of these rumble strips, I went onto the highway to go around them.

Shortly, I will be visiting Jakob and his family. He is an awesome young man, and when you meet him, you cannot help but pour your heart out to him. I can't wait to get hugs and spend time with the family.

Day 27

Sunday, August 19; Fargo, ND to Fergus Falls, MN; Daily Miles 81; Total Miles 1698. End destination Minnesota!

We left Fargo, ND, at 8 a.m. in the rain. First day since we started that we experienced RAIN. I had a strong north tailwind that

made the ride more enjoyable, but at times, it was hard to see through my glasses due to the rain. It rained hard for about 2 ½ hours and stopped by 11ish. It looked like the rest of the day would just be overcast, but it started to rain again right after lunch, and it rained all day. Everything was wet.

I stopped at a local roadside farmers market just before lunch to buy some fruit, but they only had vegetables and a melon. The owner recognized me: "You are the guy I saw on TV last night. I remember the flag about Jakob." We had a great talk, and both guys gave me a small donation. Before I left, they stuffed two carrots and a melon into my bag.

Picture of a buffalo head available at the stand and the two guys running it.

A little later, I stopped at a local restaurant to eat. I parked my bike where I could keep an eye on it. As I sat down to eat, a lady customer came up to me, "I saw you on TV last night - your meal is paid for."

Then, as I was riding in the rain, a guy pulled over ahead of me. "I saw you on TV last night." He gave me a donation; I just cannot believe how many people are willing to help Jakob. It truly is amazing. I got to Fergus Falls, MN, about 6 p.m.

DAY 28

Monday, August 20; Fergus Falls, MN to Melrose, MN; Daily Total 85; Trip Total 1783. We left Fergus Falls at 8 a.m. The weather was cool – great for riding. There was a rail trail from Fergus Falls to Melrose that took you through some nice backcountry.

Interestingly, this rail trail had a total service kiosk-type station at the beginning where you could inflate your tires, etc. It was called a bike fixation deluxe public work stand. I have never seen anything like that before, and it sure would be nice to see this at the beginning and end of all bike trails.

Going down this trail to Melrose was terrific. The trail was of crushed gravel and great to ride on. The scenery was incredible, and at times, it looked like you were riding in a tunnel of trees.

I also got a call from another TV station wanting to do an interview over the phone. This will be set up in the next couple of days. The weather was now very nice to ride in, and since I was able to reduce the weight to only two bags on the rear wheel, it was a more enjoyable ride. However, I can see the value and importance of having all four bags for long trips, as it just gives you more supplies for all occasions. All in all, it was a good day to ride.

> **Thoughts for the Day:** I am actually feeling pretty good, especially since I am four weeks into a two-month ride! I have discovered this: if you want to lose weight, ride a bike 6-8 hours a day for 60-90 miles. You WILL lose weight! ☺

DAY 29

Tuesday, August 21; Melrose, MN to Milaca, MN; Daily Miles 70; Total Miles 1853.

We left Melrose at 9 a.m. and headed to Milaca, MN. The day started out cool but warmed up in the afternoon. We followed the rail trail for approximately 30 miles and then the highway as outlined on our cycling maps. On this leg of the rail trail, we met several people who were enjoying their bikes and using the trail.

We also chanced upon one of the cyclists we had previously encountered several days ago in Circle, MT. What are the chances of running into him again on the same path when we departed at different times? He was riding east on the same route to Maine. We asked if he wanted to ride with us for a time and so now we are a threesome riding together.

I now understand why they call this state the state of 10,000 lakes - they are everywhere. This truly is a duck hunter's and fisherman's paradise. I think I will try to come back here someday for a great hunting and fishing experience.

Now, here is something AMAZING that happened. I was about 5 miles from Milaca riding by myself and heard my cell beep. The call was timely as I really needed to rest. So, I stopped to look at my text message, and it was from my friend, Chris Cuvar.

Chris often checked in with me during my ride and encouraged me. He was also well aware of Jan's medical condition, and his background as a paramedic gave me peace of mind knowing he was touching base with Jan almost daily. The text message was a true blessing to me. As I was reading it, I looked down, and there was a wooden cross with three nails embedded in it on the gravel - one on each cross arm and one on the lower

post!

What are the chances of finding a cross like this right when I needed a rest and got a text from Chris? This was again a sign from God that He was with me on my RIDE FOR JAKOB. I will carry this on my bike for the rest of the trip and never forget that moment. It could have been very easy to have ridden by it, ignored it, or never even seen it. YET, I stopped right there where it was on the side of the road.

Now, the story doesn't end there. I got to the motel where we were going to spend the night. Both Jim and Steve, our new riding partner, had already arrived and checked in. When I saw them, I was like, "Guys, you are not going to believe what I found along the side of the road just lying in the dirt." Before I could tell them what I found, they answered, "I know what you found. I saw it and rode past it." Can you believe that? Who would ride by a cross like this?

I have come to believe that this cross was a blessing from God meant for me! He has been with me on this whole RIDE FOR JAKOB and He wasn't going to let me forget that.

Tomorrow, we will enter Wisconsin. The only physical issue I am having trouble with is my fingers on my left hand. Off and on throughout the ride, they have gone numb. I think this is due to the angle of my wrists on the handlebars.

Day 30

Wednesday, August 22; Milaca, MN to St. Croix Falls, WI; Daily Miles 74; Total Miles 1927. This will be the beginning of traveling back and forth between Minnesota and Wisconsin as we follow the Mississippi River. We ended up staying in St. Croix Falls, WI.

Again, it was a cool day and great for riding. My sister, Lois, made contact with the local police and fire department. They were going to provide lodgings at the local volunteer fire hall, but this changed when the police office manager called her church, and the pastor paid for our hotel accommodations at the Delles House Motel in St. Croix Falls. Another huge blessing.

I had some challenges with my bike's left pedal and couldn't release the clip-on shoe. My bike had also fallen over again, and a few things needed adjustments. I found a bike shop in Osceola, WI, and got a complete service overhaul and a new chain as well.

This was Mennonite country. I passed several horses and carriages. It was awesome seeing families all traveling together and how they did their business as usual.

At the end of the day, I saw I had to climb a very steep, heavily trafficked four-lane road to get there. I was a little concerned about riding my bike in traffic until I discovered a walking trail that you could walk or ride on. I walked most of it, and what a relief it was to get to the top, the motel, and the end of another day.

Day 31

Thursday, August 23; St. Croix Falls, WI to Red Wing, MN; Daily Miles 74; Total Miles 2001. NOW over 2000 miles. We left at 9 a.m., going south following the St. Croix River to the Mississippi.

This was a hard ride. There were lots of long, steep hills to climb and a strong headwind all day. I hadn't experienced a headwind until now. By the end of the day, I had been on my bike for 10 ½ hours.

I went through the Taylor Falls, MN area, which is a scenic area along the St. Croix River. There are lots of marinas, and it is definitely a summer tourist area. I also came across an area called Diamond Bluff. It reminded me of the Niagara Escarpment in Ontario.

When I got to Prescott, Wisconsin, I met six bikers (motorcycle guys) from a group helping vets, and I took a picture with them. I offered, "I'd ride with you, but I think I'd only slow them down." (You think?)

I thought I was out of the mountains and hills to climb but apparently not. As I crossed the river and went back to the Minnesota side, I saw the Mississippi River Paddle-wheeler boat.

Cool! I found out this is a scenic river cruise line that you can take from the Gulf of Mexico to at least this area. I need to find out more details on this for a vacation trip.

Somewhere along today's ride, I lost a bolt from my left clip-on shoe. I don't know why the left side is having so many issues. It is more difficult to pedal, and I hope to find a bike shop soon to get it fixed again.

Day 32

Friday, August 24; Red Wing, MN to Winona, MN; Daily Miles 73; Total Miles 2074. We left this morning at 8:30 a.m. It was very overcast, with a strong indication of rain as we rode south.

Sure enough, about an hour into the ride, it rained. We were dressed for it, but you still got wet. A cold, wet mist hung in all day, penetrating your clothing and at times making the ride miserable.

As I rode along the Mississippi River, I was amazed at how wide it was. It still amazes me; you just can't imagine the width until you see it in person. Now I can see why there are scenic riverboat cruises this far from the mouth of the Mississippi River. It was a beautiful area to ride, and again, I was so blessed to be able to see and experience this part of America. I would not have normally been able to see these sites without this opportunity.

I stopped in Wabasha, a small town along the Mississippi River that had a bike shop. I got new cleats for my clip-on shoes and replaced the left bolt I had lost yesterday. I rode all morning with no cleat on my left shoe, and it made the ride slower and uncomfortable as my foot kept sliding off the pedal.

Once fixed, I was able to make up some lost time as we wanted to end the day at Winona, which was another 35 miles down the road. We could not wait to get into a motel to get warm, dry, and wash all of our clothes. I can't really complain, though, as this was only the second day we had to ride in the rain.

All other days, it was the HEAT that got to us. My cell got wet again, making it difficult to take pictures. We would have liked to have gone further today, but we were just too cold and wet to continue. We were still a trio as our new riding friend Steve stayed with us and helped share in the cost of the motel room.

DAY 33

Saturday, August 25; Winona, MN to Kendall, WI; Daily Miles 73; Total Miles 2147. We left this morning at 8:30 a.m. and headed for Reedsburg but only got to Kendall, WI.

It was a good day for riding; nice and sunny. Our ride took us to a gravel bike path for some 49 miles today. We had to purchase a Trail Pass for $5 and were not expecting that, but o'well. This was an old rail trail that was 55 miles long in total, which we will continue to follow tomorrow. We crossed the Mississippi River into Wisconsin again and are now traveling east. We won't be crossing back into Minnesota again.

The old rail line led us through three long mountain tunnels, one being almost a mile long with no lights. We had to walk our bikes through with our headlights on. It was nice getting off the main highways for a change. We met a lot of bikers on this old trail throughout the day.

BIKES MUS
BE WALKED
THRU TUNNEL
KEEP RIGHT
SINGLE FILE

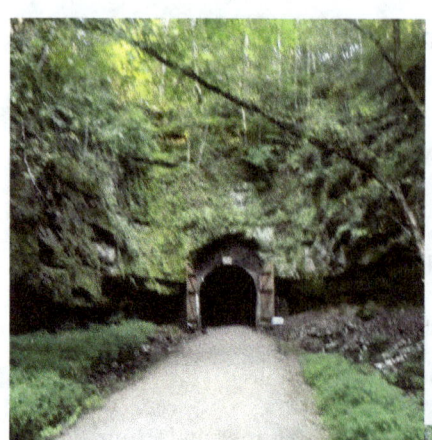

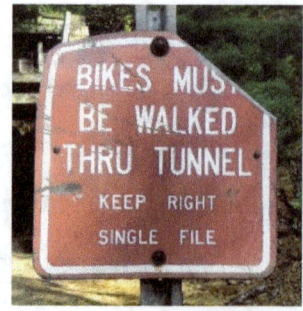

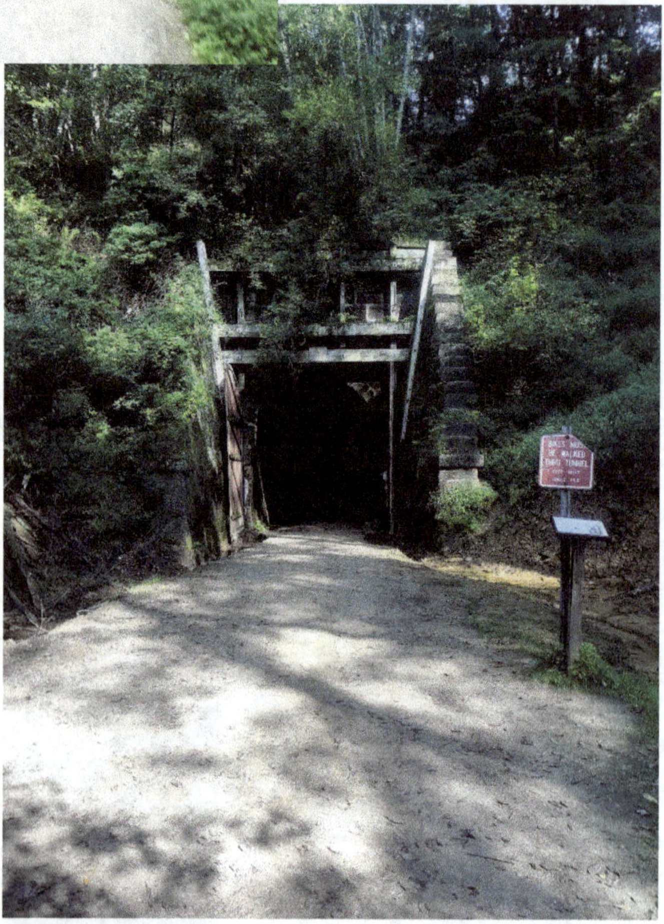

We came to Sparta, a small town whose claim to fame was 'the bicycling capital of America.' Apparently, this is where the bicycles with the large front wheels and smaller back wheels were manufactured. I got a picture taken with one of those photo displays,  and my name was Ben Bikin. Funny, but a great picture.

As I was walking my bike through one of the long tunnels, it was dark and wet, and you had to have your headlight and flasher going so you would not fall or hit anything. As I was walking, a guy passed me, and it was Steve. I left him in Sparta some miles back, and he just now caught up to me. We chatted a bit, and both agreed to continue the ride together. That turned out to be another wonderful blessing.

We spent the night in Kendall, WI, where our three riding partners split up as a team. Jim was headed down a different route.

Steve and I planned to catch the ferry from Milwaukee to Muskegon, MI. Then, Steve would go his own route, and I would go home to Grand Rapids for a few days. After that, I would continue on through Michigan to Ontario, New York, and Massachusetts.

DAY 34

Sunday, August 26; Kendall, WI to Sauk City, WI; Daily Miles 65; Total Miles 2212. We left at 7:30 a.m. this morning, wanting to get off earlier than normal.

The day started out sunny and cool. The weather report, however, showed a large bad weather pattern moving in, so we should expect something during the day.

I had bad fall #4, on my bike. We came up fast behind a couple who stopped on the trail, and I could not unclip either shoe. I hit the brakes, and over I went, trying to miss running into them. I cut my arm and leg, but overall, I wasn't seriously injured. The guy took my camera and got a picture of me under my bike. I think I am going to change to a cage-type pedal for the last leg of this ride. These falls hurt!

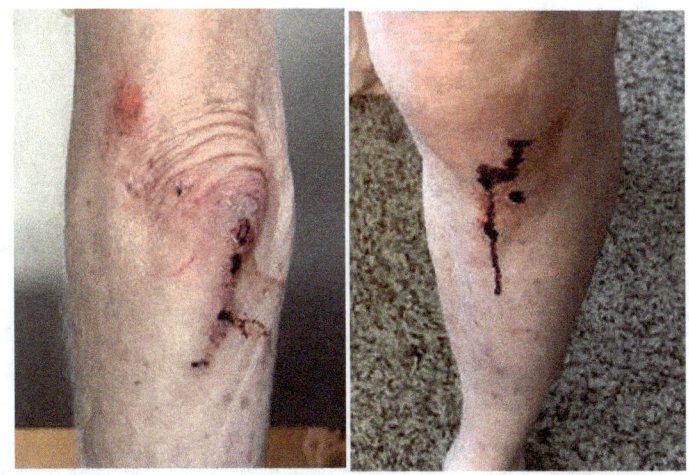

Well, it did rain, and it rained hard. At times, I couldn't see the road ahead of me. What I did see was lightning touching down all over the place. This went on for over HALF an hour, then it stopped.

The road surface was very slippery, making it difficult to go downhill. Not to mention the poor visibility with cars and trucks passing. I stopped at another bike shop and got my pedals adjusted again. We have at least two more days traveling in Wisconsin and should arrive in Muskegon, MI, late Tuesday night. Then, home in Grand Rapids late Wednesday afternoon. I CAN'T wait to see Jan!

DAY 35

Monday, August 27; Sauk City, WI to Johnson Creek, WI; Daily Miles 65; Total Miles 2277. We left at 7:30 a.m. today, and tomorrow night, Muskegon, MI (maybe?).

Again, we found ourselves trying to get ahead of any expected bad weather. It was a good day for riding, but rather muggy and

humid. The navigational route that I had on my maps was rather confusing. I am thankful for Steve, my new riding partner, who kept us on the correct bike route. We had to go down several back county roads, not all going east toward Milwaukee, but I just put my faith in his navigational skills.

We finally got to the Glacial Drumlin State Trail, which took us to Johnson Creek.

This was a shortcut, so to speak, that would take us many miles further tomorrow.

All along this trail, we experienced many fallen trees due to the bad storm/weather and wind we experienced yesterday. We had to lift our bikes over several trees that fell across the bike trail.

This should be our last night's stay in Wisconsin. The plan is to get up early and go to Milwaukee in time for the last ferry to Muskegon, MI. We want to be there by 6 p.m. I also did an interview with the Johnson Creek newspaper about my RIDE FOR JAKOB.

DAY 36

Tuesday, August 28; Johnson Creek, WI to Milwaukee, WI; Daily Miles 61; Total Miles 2338. Today was an interesting day. Our plan was to go to Milwaukee, knowing we could make the 7:30 p.m. ferry crossing to Muskegon, MI.

The weather report did not look good at all, and we knew it was going to be a hard ride with rain, wind, and down trees along the Glacial Drumlin State Trail. It was overcast when we left, but the sun came out, and we had NO rain or wind the entire morning.

We went down the gravel trail and encountered many trees that had fallen across the trail, making it very difficult to get any speed or distance. I almost fell again because it was slippery with mud. I went into many slides, making it difficult to keep my bike from going over.

We finally hit a trail block that was so big we couldn't really get around it. So, we decided to leave the trail, push our bikes through a large ditch, and take the county road going east toward Milwaukee. Getting off that trail and on the paved county road was a good idea.

Once we got to the county road, the weather turned sunny and warm. We saw the possibility that we could make the 12-noon ferry, but it was going to be a push. That being said, we stepped up our speed to a consistent ride at 15 mph, compared to the average 10 mph.

I was having a hard time keeping up the pace to ensure that we got to the ferry dock by noon. I was OK with the 7:30 departure, but since I did not have this trail map, I had to make it happen. My partner went ahead of me, but thankfully, he was waiting at the next crucial turn. That made me feel much better, as I knew he wanted me to make this noon crossing.

As we went through Milwaukee, I had no idea where we were. The pace was increased to nearly 20 mph on the odometer, and that was a real push, but I was able to keep up with him. It was a hard ride for me, going through several main streets in Milwaukee, which was also an experience.

We arrived at the ferry dock 15 minutes before departure. That was close! It felt great to sit back, relax, and enjoy the ride. I planned to get to the Kentwood Fire Station tomorrow at 4:30 p.m. After that, I'd be home for a week before heading out for the final leg of my RIDE FOR JAKOB.

After many miles of riding together, it will be an adjustment when Steve leaves. He has been a blessing in so many ways, but I don't worry about finishing the journey on my own. In fact, I think it might feel nice to ride at a pace that suits me better.

Day 37

Wednesday, August 29; Muskegon, MI to Kentwood, MI; Daily Miles 61; Total Miles 2399. Hey, only another 1000 miles to go!

We got up early so we could each make our various connections. Steve parted company on another route that would take him on a more direct path to the east side of Michigan. I found the starting point of the Musketawa Trail, which took me to Grand Rapids. I liked this trail as it was paved the entire length, making riding much easier. As I arrived in Walker, I was met by the Fox 17 news people who wanted to do a live interview as I arrived in the Grand Rapids area. That was awesome, and I am sure I gave them a lot to report.

When I got to the Rivertown Crossing area on 44th Street, I stopped at a gas station to get some water, and a police officer drove slowly by me, looking at my sign about Jakob. It was 2:37 p.m., and I had to make sure I arrived at the Kentwood Fire Station between 4:30 and 5 p.m. My family was going to meet me there, and I could not wait to see them. I was not expecting what happened next.

As I was riding down 52nd Street near the intersection of Kalamazoo, a police car again rode by me and just looked at me as he passed. The next thing I knew, he had circled around behind me and pulled me over. He told me that the various police departments were watching for me and that I should pull over at the parking lot of the church on the corner.

As I rode my bike into the parking lot, I saw another police cruiser waiting. After I had a nice talk with them, they explained that one cruiser would go ahead of me, and the second cruiser would follow behind with their lights flashing. Wow, what a feeling! People began honking and waving as they approached and passed me.

I rode into the Kentwood Fire Station right at 5:00 p.m., and there was my family and a number of friends.

The grandchildren were all excited to see me and ran up to me on the bike. But I knew before I could hug any of them, I needed to hug my wife. I would never have attempted this ride without Jan's support, love, and prayers. I gave her a BIG KISS, and all I could say was, "I sure missed you, and thank you for your prayers!"

As my grandchildren jumped around me, waiting for their turn for hugs, one of them asked, "Grandpa, are you a hero or something?" As I looked around at the press, firefighters, Police, and people, I can tell you I sure felt like a hero.

I had another live interview at the station, and I thanked all the Kentwood Firemen for allowing us to host my arrival.

I had decided to take the next week off to get some R&R, spend my anniversary with my wife, and repack and redesign my travel bags for the next leg of the trip across Michigan, Ontario, New York, and Massachusetts. I had learned a lot and knew I could make some valuable adjustments to my gear.

DAY 38

One week later. Wednesday, September 5; Grand Rapids, MI to St. Johns, MI; Daily Miles 61; Total Miles 2460.

Well, I am off on the last leg of the RIDE FOR JAKOB. I had a great rest for a week in Grand Rapids. Yesterday, September 4th, was our wedding anniversary, and we celebrated a wonderful 31 years of marriage. I cannot even express what this was going to mean for Jakob, Jason, Sue, and Brooklynn. I needed her, and all that is a part of our relationship.

Today was a very good day to ride. The weather was warm and hot at times, but the sky was mostly overcast and cooler. I left Grand Rapids from the main fire station downtown and had a great send-off. All the firefighters were there, and we got a wonderful group picture.

This was the hall that, through Fire Inspector Bill Smith, started the entire firefighter support program. The letter signed by the GR Fire Department Fire Chief opened doors for us to find accommodations in many of the states we went through. A BIG THANK YOU goes out to the Chiefs and those in Grand Rapids who supported me and the RIDE FOR JAKOB.

I finally rolled into St. John's to rest for the night. The Clinton Area Ambulance Service in St. John's allowed me to pitch my tent behind their Ambulance outlet. This was the first time I had used my tent to camp along the bike route, and it was supposed to rain.

I will be in the Flint, MI, area tomorrow, but will find a city on the other side of Flint to stay the night. I also discovered a rail trail that I can ride tomorrow from St John's to Flint. M-21 was a good highway to ride on. It was a good day and the first day of the final 1000 miles, and I did it solo!

Day 39

Thursday, September 6; St. Johns, MI to Flint, MI; Daily Miles 53; Total Miles 2513. I left at 8 a.m. after having a wonderful breakfast provided by the Ambulance staff.

The rail trail I wanted to take started here in St. Johns and would take me to Flint. It sure made for much easier riding. The trail was fully paved, and again, another great day for a ride.

I got a call from a radio station in London, Ontario, who heard about my RIDE FOR JAKOB, and they knew I was going to be riding through London. We talked for about 30 minutes, and they said they were going to air our interview either today or when I arrived.

I was in contact with my friend Chris, who said he would meet me in Flint. We chose a location at a local mall parking lot. It sure was nice to see him and to spend the evening just catching up on events, etc. Chris explained that riding through Flint was not a good idea, especially at that time of the day. Especially trying to get to the specific destination I wanted to end my day at. He was right; the traffic was very heavy. A BIG THANK YOU goes out to Chris for looking after me today.

We had a lot of laughs as we are old friends, and like always, we had lots of stories to share.

DAY 40

Friday, September 7; Flint, MI to Wallaceburg, ON; Daily Miles 52; Total Miles 2565. Today took me 10 hours, far too long for 52 miles.

I got on a rail trail that took me south to Rochester, MI, and not east, for 15 miles. In the end, I got on another trail that took me northeast, but well out of my way and miles I didn't need to do. When I discovered I was going the wrong way, I met a guy who directed me to Highway 23 going east to New Baltimore and was supposed to save me a lot of time. Wrong!

The distance was only 8 miles, but loose gravel made it very difficult to control my bike. So, I walked at least 6 of the 8 miles, and that just slowed me down even more. I had to stay off the highway because the traffic was too busy, and people kept honking their horns at me. So, I had to walk.

When I finally got to New Baltimore, the shoulder was designed for cyclists, and I made up as much time as possible. I got to Algonac at 5:30 p.m., took the ferry to Canada, Walpole Island, and arrived in Wallaceburg at 6:15 p.m.

My sister had contacted the Wallaceburg Fire Department, and they opened their doors to me. They are an awesome bunch of guys. Several knew my son, Jason Smith, from London, Ontario.

It was great sharing about my ride across the US and what was in store for me across Ontario and back into the States. The firemen made a fantastic dinner. They sure can cook! In the morning, with the crew change, they made me a wonderful breakfast and sent me on my way. Thanks a bunch, guys.

> **Thoughts for the Day:** I have eaten pretty well along this journey, but I will admit that many of my meals were the TruPlenish shakes from Mannatech. Even though I had lost some weight, my appetite was good, and I quickly found I could really put away the food as these firefighters knew how to feed you!

DAY 41

Saturday, September 8; Wallaceburg, ON, to a SURPRISE near Longwood, ON!

The firemen escorted me out of town to Highway 2, heading toward London. The weather was good, but I had a strong headwind for the entire ride.

As I was riding along Highway #2, I saw another cyclist ahead of me also fighting the wind. I was very impressed as this was a man older than me, in his late 70s, who, a year ago, left Seattle, WA, and followed the same route I had just traveled. He told me that he got to Minneapolis, MN, last year and got hit by a car that totaled his bike and put him in the hospital for a few days. He decided to return home to Maine for the rest of that year but picked up his ride this year from where he stopped in Minneapolis.

We talked for a while, and then I was on my way again after we wished each other a safe trip. Meeting other bikers, especially those older than me, just spurred me on.

I had a little incident. A bee hit my helmet and got inside through one of the air vents. It just kept moving around inside my helmet. It took me a minute to find a safe place to stop and take off my helmet. When I finally got my helmet off, the bee flew out and, fortunately, did not sting my head. Phew, that was a close one!

I traveled on familiar country roads, calling my son, Jason, to tell him where I was and that I was going to be going through Delaware, Ontario, where he first worked at the volunteer fire department. I was almost to Delaware when Jason and Jakob pulled up alongside me!

I wasn't expecting that. I almost started to cry; I did tear up some. Jakob came over immediately and grabbed my hand. WOW, what a surprise! Words cannot even express the emotions.

So, we marked the spot where we met, put my bike in the back of Jason's truck, and went to his house for the night. To make it even more of a surprise, Jan and her sister were there! I couldn't believe it. What a wonderful family reunion in a place we once called home.

I have to admit, it was nice to finally get out of the strong wind I had been facing all day.

Day 42

Sunday, September 9; Longwood, ON to London, ON; Daily Miles 41; Total Miles 2606.

I restarted my ride on Highway #2 to continue to London, Ontario proper. The Delaware Fire Department met me first, and it was a great reception. My son Jason, who was a firefighter in Delaware at one time, arranged this.

I was escorted by a fire truck to Komoka, where I was again met by a large group of people and another London fire truck, which gave me another personal escort 6 miles to Byron (London) at station #12.

What was also exciting was that a number of firefighters who were also cyclists and friends of Jason met me in Komoka, and we all rode as a group to the fire station. This was AWESOME!

I could not believe the reception. So many people were there, friends, relatives, my mother, Jan and her sister, firefighters and JAKOB! A day I will never forget. Jakob is getting a lot of attention from people all across the US and Canada.

Balloons were flying and two large cakes were served to all. There were approximately 100 people, all gathered at the fire station to welcome me and the riders as we followed the fire truck with lights flashing.

I cannot say enough about the firefighter associations in the US and Canada and their support in raising funds for Jakob and opening their doors for lodging and help - THANKS, GUYS! I stayed in London on Monday, then continued to cross Ontario, heading for Buffalo, NY, on Tuesday morning.

Thoughts for the Day: Now 6 weeks of riding my bike. Many people have asked me, "How are you feeling after six weeks on the road?" When I really had the time to stop and think about it, I found I was asking myself, "How and why am I not experiencing the fatigue that would be a normal expectation? How can I explain how good I feel?"

All I could come up with was that I made it a point and priority to take the Ambrotose Life nutrient supplement every day. I realized over the course of my journey and the occasional missed dose, the IMPORTANCE of taking the supplement and never missing a day. I knew these products were working for me, and the difference when I missed a day. Therefore, I could only come to one conclusion—MANNATECH PRODUCTS WORK!

Day 43

Monday, September 10.

A day of rest to visit with my mother, Jason, Sue, granddaughter Brooklynn, and Jakob.

I was presented with a wonderful work of art, a painting showing the firefighter badge, and signed by all that were there. This will hang on my wall for a long time.

Day 44

Tuesday, September 11; London, ON to Simcoe, ON; Daily Miles 65; Total Miles 2671. I hit the road again at 8 a.m., heading for Tillsonburg, Ontario, about 50 miles from London, and then two more nights in Ontario.

I left London from Fire Station #11 in Lambeth/London, and was sent off by the firefighters there. Thanks, guys, for your support. It was a good day for a ride.

I traveled through the area/country where I once lived and followed a few back roads to cut cross-country to Highway #3. This would eventually take me to Fort Erie and Buffalo, NY. However, I

decided not to get onto Highway #3. Instead, I followed some less-traveled county roads all the way to Simcoe, Ontario. Traveling through this part of Ontario brought back great memories as I once lived in this part of South Western Ontario. I did make one wrong turn and went 4 miles out of my way. Oh well, I'm sure it won't be the last time.

The weather was great for riding, with little to no wind but cool temperatures. The local radio station in Simcoe asked me to stop in before I left in the morning for a possible radio interview.

DAY 45

Wednesday, September 12; Simcoe, ON to Dunnville, ON; Daily Miles 51; Total Miles 2722. I'm going to follow the coastline of Lake Erie to Port Colborne. Today will be a longer day of riding.

I left Simcoe a little later than normal, but the day started out well. I found a rail trail from Simcoe to Port Dover and made some good time. I also discovered a road that followed the lake (Lake Erie), and it was a beautiful ride with a great view of the lake, but it became a little confusing. I made a BIG mistake and turned the wrong way. That took me some 10 miles in the wrong direction. I stopped an OPP police car to get directions. So, back then, I went in the same direction. Oh well!

However, it is amazing how things turn out. A lady (Liz) stopped me along the highway, "I just read about you in the paper." She invited me to have lunch with her, her son, and her son-in-law. WOW, what a blessing! She also donated to Jakob's Ride. Lesson learned: even when you make a mistake, you never know what will develop because of it or how God will use it for good.

I again followed the lake road, but now I was almost 2 hours behind. I knew I wouldn't make Port Colborne for the night. I was also carrying more weight than previously since I had restocked, and it slowed me down. Plus, I had a moderate headwind all day. Dunnville sure looked good for the night.

It will be a stretch to get to Fort Erie tomorrow, so I will be leaving very early in the morning.

Day 46

Thursday, September 13; Dunnville, ON to Fort Erie, ON; Daily Miles 47; Total Miles 2769. I thought I had a potentially long ride today, so I left at 6:45 a.m. and took the Lake Shore Highway.

It was a little longer ride, but I decided to stay off the main Highway #3. It was a great ride, with no traffic, no wind, and very few hills to climb. I made it to Port Colborne in 2 hours!! So, I stopped for a good breakfast. People saw Jakob's sign and had lots of questions. Right after I left Pt Colborne, I found a trail called "the friendship trail' totally paved, and it went all the way to Ft. Erie. It was awesome. I met lots of other cyclists in large groups. This trail is well-known and well-kept.

When I was leaving the restaurant after breakfast, the guy I met just outside of Wallaceburg was stopping at the same restaurant for breakfast. He was cycling from Minneapolis, MN. It was interesting that we were on the same bike route, but he took Highway #3, which I stayed off of. He agreed it was not a good road to ride on, but that was the route outlined on his maps. Since I knew the roads in Ontario, it gave me an advantage to choose a much safer route.

I had already finished my breakfast, but we had a nice chat. I was impressed with his dream to ride across the U.S. from Seattle, WA, to his destination in Maine, and he was close to 80 years old. How cool is that? I am going to make as many long-distance rides as I can in the future years. Thanks, bud, for the encouragement.

As I was riding along the trail, a guy passed me and came back. He saw the firefighter emblem, and he asked a lot of questions. Come to find out, he worked at the same fire station in Mississauga where my son Jason started his career as a firefighter. Since I was not sure of the route to the Peace Bridge and customs, he rode with me to show me the way. He also helped me find where my motel was for the night. Again, I kept meeting great people along the ride.

I got a call from a local newspaper reporter who wanted to do an interview with me when I got to Ft Erie. We had a great interview. Sona Vanderhoof from Mannatech also visited me, she drove from Markham, Ontario, to meet with me, have dinner, and do a live Facebook interview. WOW, it was wonderful! Another huge BLESSING. I feel that great things are going to happen for Jakob and his future security.

Tomorrow, I cross into the US at Buffalo, NY, and get on the Erie Canalway trail, which is 360 miles long and takes me to Albany, NY. I will be on it for a few days. I am watching the weather forecast, and I am expecting a wet ride over the next few days, but I am ready.

Day 47

Friday, September 14; Fort Erie, ON to Albion, NY; Daily Miles 76; Total Miles 2845. I left this morning at 8 a.m. and crossed the Peace Bridge into Buffalo, NY.

The walk and cycle bridge over the canal was under construction, so I had to call for a shuttle van that customs arranged to cross over into the U.S. Then, I found the Erie Canalway trail to start my ride across the state of New York.

This trail was great to travel on, not all paved but I felt much safer knowing I was off any major highway. The number of cyclists, runners, and people out walking along the Erie Canal was impressive.

The canal itself was nice to follow and in some cities, boats were going through the locks. The weather was warm and sunny, but tomorrow, with the hurricane hitting the Carolinas, they say this part of the U.S. should experience rain. I hope not for at least another few days.

Again, several people stopped me for information about Jakob. When I got to Albion, I had an interview with a local newspaper. Again, I met several cyclists loaded with bags who were doing long-distance rides. Unless you get on a trail, you don't generally see many people doing these long rides, and I was surprised at the number of folks involved in this sport/adventure riding. I'm looking forward to tomorrow's ride. Feeling good, no aches or pains, and still running strong. The Erie Canal is a great area to see and visit.

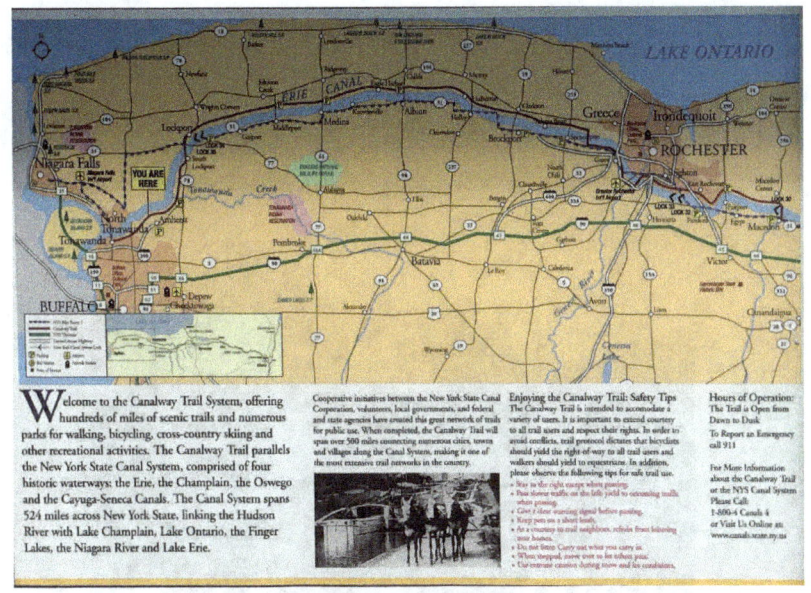

DAY 48

Saturday, September 15; Albion, NY to Palmyra, NY; Daily Miles 68; Total Miles 2913. Rode on the Erie Canal Trail.

My daughter, Kyra Jacobs, was one of my Guardian Angels who followed me every day and used an app called Life360. I will never forget some of the funny things that happened because of my 'Eyes in the Sky,' as I called it.

I had just stopped at a traffic light after entering Rochester, NY, and was wondering which way to go when I met these two other cyclists who lived in Rochester. I told them my story and how I was trying to get to the Atlantic Ocean. They offered to ride with me through the city of Rochester to make sure I found my way. Another Blessing!

"Before we go through the city, though, we would like to take you to one of our favorite pit stops for some ice cream." They weren't going to get any argument from me. I love ice cream. So, I was like, "Let's do it!"

Now, keep in mind that Kyra is tracking me using her app but has no idea what is actually happening on the ground. All she sees is that suddenly I'm no longer going straight but have turned left taking me towards the local hospital.

So, as I was riding along with my new friends, I got a call. Kyra is in somewhat of a panic. "WHY didn't you keep going straight? Are you headed to the hospital? Were you in an accident?" I reassured her all was well and that I was only going to eat 'ice cream.' I had no idea the road I was on took me to the hospital!

Now, here is just one more funny of the 360 app. I was on a long highway stretch and had to go to the bathroom - nature does call, you know! With no restroom around, I had to leave the road and walk into the woods for privacy. I was barely done with my business when Kyra called, 'What happened? Are you okay?' Talk about embarrassing; I can't even go to the toilet without being watched - so to speak.

I laugh now, but in truth, it sure felt good to know that my daughter was keeping an eye on me and that if something did happen, someone would know.

DAY 49

Sunday, September 16; Palmyra, NY to Syracuse, NY; Daily Miles 76; Total Miles 2989. I left at 7 a.m. and got onto the trail just at daybreak.

When the sun came up, it was difficult to see the conditions of the trail as the sun was hitting my eyes, and I almost fell off my bike twice. The trail was quite confusing at times as it did not follow the canal in some areas. The route took me on county roads, and in some small towns, the path was not well marked. Fortunately, my GPS kept me on track. My original plan was to get as close to Syracuse as possible for the day, and then tomorrow, I would take my time to go through the city. I was told it was going to be very busy and, again, somewhat confusing.

About 20 miles into the ride, I met a father and son who were also riding the Erie Canalway trail from Buffalo to Albany, NY. They invited me to ride along with them for as far as I wanted to join them. I agreed, and they invited me to have lunch with them. As we discussed the rest of the day's journey, they told me they were going to not only go *to* Syracuse but *through* it today. So, my ride plans changed.

I have to admit that I felt more comfortable going through cities with a riding partner vs. doing it on my own. I'm sure I would have been fine, but it ended up being a good decision even though I was adding another 20 miles to my day's ride. Besides, I had only done 50 miles that day, so my ending miles would be 76. I could do that!

We came into Syracuse at 3:30 in the afternoon with virtually no traffic downtown, wow! We made it through the city quite fast, but again, the trail markings were almost nonexistent. It was like three blind mice following each other, but  we did it. We got to the motel, where I decided to stay for the night at 5 p.m. That means that I was on my bike for about 10 hours today.

I've talked about setting a goal, having a dream, a vision, and a purpose. My driving force and purpose every day is JAKOB! My ride, I believe, will make a difference in his future life and security. The radio interview by Mike Stubbs in London, Ontario, CFPL 980, says it all. If you haven't heard it, please take the time to listen to my interview with him. Also, check out the TV interview by Fox 17, which followed me along my route to Grand Rapids. Both completely outline my WHY!

My goal was to raise $100,000 for Jakob. Each day that I rode closer to the end of this journey and to the Atlantic Ocean, I chose to believe that JAKOB would be BLESSED no matter what the total raised!

Day 50

Monday, September 17; Syracuse, NY to Utica, NY; Daily Miles 75; Total Miles 3064. Today is a day of accomplishment – I went over the 3,000 mile marker! WOW!!! I had a great ride today.

First thing in the morning is a nice time to start; it's cool but a little foggy. Fall is really starting to show its colors here in this part of New York, and leaves are falling on the trail. As much as this looks nice, it's creating a dangerous situation. Leaves are now covering some parts of the trail, making it difficult to see potholes and obstacles. I move along quite fast on both gravel and paved surfaces

and when you hit a hole, etc., it makes it difficult to control the bike. I hit a pothole quite hard today, and it knocked off both saddle bags on the front of my bike. That shakes you up. I started to slow my riding pace as much as possible.

I rode solo today but did meet several people along the canal route. I am getting closer to the end of the New York Erie Canalway trail. At least another two days in New York. Tomorrow, they say it's going to rain. If it does, I will take a rest day, as I have been hitting the trails and roads hard for the past 2 weeks.

Day 51

Tuesday, September 18; Utica, NY to Schenectady, NY; Daily Miles 84; Total Miles 3148.

Today was an interesting day. Based on the weather report, I was going to stay in Utica and just get some rest because of the rain projection, but when I looked outside at 7:30 a.m., there was no rain in sight. A little overcast but warm, so I decided to forget the rest and hit the road. I had no set destination planned, but maybe somewhere about 50 miles would be good. Excellent day for a ride.

During my ride today, I met two guys who were doing the same ride as I was, from Oregon. I stopped and chatted with the first one. He commented on the heat that we had experienced throughout our ride and how it had affected him. We had a lot to share and it was an enjoyable respite. The other guy I met was just down the trail a ways further. He was also on the same route from Oregon. His goal for today was to get to Schenectady, NY, but that was going to be another 40 miles yet to travel. Forty more miles, did I want to do it - why

not! So, we rode together the rest of the day for a total of 84 miles. For a planned day of rest - it felt good to get these extra miles behind me. Tomorrow is another day. The weather looks good, so who knows what will happen?

I just found out that the distance to Revere, MA, is about 220 miles, so I'm getting closer. I can smell the Atlantic Ocean from here - just kidding.

I still have mountains to cross. I took a picture of a sign that was along the trail that was very profound. It said: 'Set your goals high and don't stop until you get there!' How powerful is that, especially right now when I am that close and the second one said: 'Persistence is the key to success!' Great markers to keep you focused and keep me driving onward and to show up when I was going to stop at just 50 miles!!!!

Day 52

Wednesday, September 19; Schenectady, NY to Troy NY; Daily Miles 23; Total Miles 3171. Today was a short day.

I had to be in Albany, NY, by 10:30 a.m. to do a live TV interview for the local news10 station. They took a lot of video coverage while I was riding. Plus, I had a great interview as well. It means a lot to me to get to explain the WHY behind the RIDE FOR JAKOB. I was with them for over an hour and then had to plan my route through Troy, NY, and on into Massachusetts. My hope was to get to Revere, MA, on Sunday. Since that was going to be a push to make happen, I decided to rest the remainder of today and just review my plan well.

DAY 53

Thursday, September 20; Troy, NY to Florida, MA; Daily Miles 50; Total Miles 3221. I started at 8 a.m. and stopped at a local fire department as I was riding through Troy, NY.

They wanted a picture of me with my bike in front of one of the fire trucks and more information on my RIDE FOR JAKOB. They also told me about the mountain climbs ahead and how tough they were going to be, and they were not kidding.

I thought the Rockies were bad - these climbs were very steep and long, and I had to walk and push my bike for what seemed like hours, and it was. Three people saw the TV report that was aired yesterday in Albany, and they stopped me to not only wish me a safe ride but donate for Jakob as well. I also got several message responses as well.

After a long day of riding, walking, and pushing my bike and only going 50 miles today, I was stopped by another guy who also saw the TV clip and asked me if I had a room for the night here in Florida, MA. (Oh, by the way, I am now in Massachusetts!) My plan was to go further today, but these mountain climbs just knocked me out.

He called a local motel owner to see if they had any vacancies and to see if I could get a discount. When I arrived, I was pleasantly surprised to find that my room was looked after for the evening. It's hard to describe your feelings when so many people say how this ride has touched them. All I can say is THANK YOU.

Also, today, after some 20 miles, my bike didn't seem right; gears were slipping, something was rubbing on the wheel, and it just felt uncomfortable, but I couldn't see or find the cause. My sister said there was a bike shop in the next town, 12 miles further. I arrived and had my bike serviced.

Somehow, I broke two spokes, the gear lever was loose, making it difficult to change gears, and one of the screws holding my rear fender in place was missing, and several nuts were loose as well. I hit a couple of bad potholes over the past few days, and the condition of my bike was showing the effects. Thankfully, everything was able to be fixed, and I am in the last stretch heading for the Atlantic. My goal is to arrive in Revere on Sunday, September 23rd, sometime after 1 p.m. I will have more details on the exact location over the next couple of days.

DAY 54

Friday, September 21; Florida, MA to Boston, MA; Daily Miles 62; Total Miles 3283. Today started in dense fog. The first really foggy day on this trip. Now, about 100 miles from the ocean! I can hardly wait.

I stayed at a motel on the summit of this mountain just outside Florida, MA. I wanted to get off early at 7 a.m., but I just could not see the road clearly in front of me, so I stopped and decided to leave at 8:30 a.m. The fog lifted some, but I knew that it would be easier to see once I got to a lower elevation. It was a cold and wet ride, and it rained most of the day. I had to wear my rain jacket and put on my leg warmers as riding was just too cold. There were lots of hills to climb, but the ride down was awesome; however, it was too wet to really get any speed. All traveling was on #2 Highway, and the traffic overall was good; not too busy.

I was pleasantly surprised when a car pulled over ahead of me and outstepped my sister, Lois, and my brother-in-law, Roger. What a surprise! Lois had tracked me all over the U.S., and she sure helped me navigate my travels. She was another of my 'Eyes in the Sky'

angels. She constantly called, "You just went the wrong way!" I have to say I think she enjoyed those calls a bit too much.

Knowing the Boston area was going to be tough, they came early to guide me to the beach through several residential areas and various major roads, welcome me to the Atlantic Ocean, and drive me back to Grand Rapids.

Day 55

Saturday, September 22; Boston, MA to Boston East Hotel; Daily Miles 45; Total Miles 3328. I started out today at 9 a.m.

The traffic coming into the Boston area was extremely difficult to navigate. Lots of side roads to keep me off the major highways. I had no set route to follow for the most part, and it took hours to find any path to travel on.

Now for another huge surprise: I got a knock at my motel door. Who should be standing there but my daughter, Kyra, my grandson, Corbin, and my son, Jason, the father of Jakob, whom this RIDE

FOR JAKOB was for? Talk about getting emotional. This was an incredible surprise; they wanted to be here in Revere when I arrived and took my bike to the Atlantic Ocean.

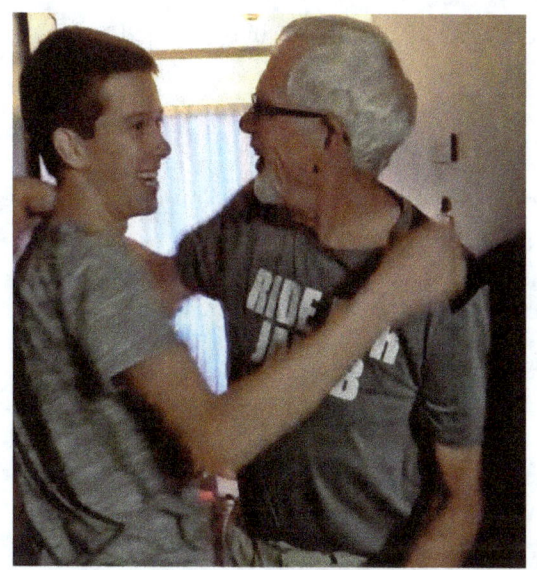

I am one BLESSED man and grandfather - WOW! Tomorrow is the day that I reach the end of my RIDE FOR JAKOB. I want to thank all of you who have supported me and donated to Jakob. I still believe my goal of financial security for Jakob will be reached.

DAY 56

Sunday, September 23; Boston, East Hotel to Revere, MA; Daily Miles 20; Total Miles 3348. A day of celebration! I cannot believe I rode my bike from the Pacific to the Atlantic Ocean. Wow!

A dream come true, and for once, I can say, 'I lived my dream awake.' The reception at the Revere beach was overwhelming, and the people who were there left me speechless!

Thanks to everyone who supported me on my RIDE FOR JAKOB. All of you have BLESSED Jakob in so many ways. We love you all. Thank you again for taking this RIDE FOR JAKOB with me. Total miles - 3502 miles from coast to coast in 56 days.

Front Wheel in the Atlantic

*Corbin, Kyra, Jason,
Ken, Lois, Roger*

Corbin, Kyra, Jason

*Sona Vanderhoof
from Mannatech*

Having Sonna from Mannatech there at the end of this journey was unbelievable. This expression of support says so much about her leadership and character. To come to see me ride into the Atlantic Ocean - I have no words to say but THANK YOU. I will never forget this. If you are interested in learning more about the products I took on this journey, I have included a section about Mannatech at the end of this book.

> **Thoughts for the Day:** I have always believed that your body can heal itself, and no matter how old you are, you can have a healthy body IF you take care of it.
>
> This journey is a living testimony of what a body can endure when given the right care. Not only did my body endure, but it thrived on this journey. When I arrived at the Atlantic, I was in the best shape of my life, and I felt AMAZING!
>
> Many people expected me to need time to recover from such a journey, but I had energy to spare. There is NO OTHER reason for such an outcome but the benefits of the vitamins and supplements Mannatech

PART 3
Reflections

TRIBUTE TO JAN

Here is my derivative of Sara Bareilles' "She Used to Be Mine":

It's not simple to say,

that most days, I don't recognize me.

It's not easy to know

that I'm not anything like I used to be.

Caring, supportive yes, although it's true

at times I wasn't as attentive as I could have been.

Jan was perfect in so many ways,

beautiful on the outside, beautiful on the inside,

a loving and faithful wife,

a supportive and caring mother

and an awesome grandmother that words cannot express.

She is gone but she used to be MINE!

It's not what I asked for

or even thought was possible as the days move along.

Sometimes life just slips in through the back door

and carves out a person that GOD knew

was the perfect GIFT, HE truly meant for you.

Life as I now know it, is not what I asked for

I know I would give so much more back to you, and a chance to
start over and re-write an ending or two
for the woman I knew, if I could.

You were reckless just enough,
you got hurt but you knew how to toughen up
when you were bruised and when you got stuck and got scared of
the life that was inside you.
I watched her get stronger each day
to fight just a little to bring back the fire in her eyes.
That's been gone but she used to be mine—used to be mine!
You don't know what it's like to lose someone, like I loved JAN!

Gone From My Sight

I am standing upon the seashore.
A ship at my side spreads her white sails to the
morning breeze and starts for the blue ocean.
She is an object of beauty and strength.
I stand and watch her until, at length she hangs like a
speck of white cloud just where the sea and the sky
come to mingle with each other.
Then someone at my side says: "There, she is gone!"
'Gone where?'

Gone from my sight. That is all.
She is just as large in mast and hull and spar as she was when she left my side, and she is just as able to bear the load of living freight to her destined port.
Her diminished size is in me, not in her.
And just at the moment when someone at my side says: "There, she is gone!" There are other eyes watching her coming, and other voices Ready to take up the glad shout, from her sleep:
"Here she comes!"

GREAT GRANDPA SMITH

How do you describe a FEELING? It is something that sometimes words just cannot express, what is inside you or your heart and mind, that just compels you and drives you to do something outside of yourself.

My father instilled in me when I was a young boy that "When you have a chance to travel and to see the world—go for it. It may seem somewhat scary and you will not feel comfortable with it, but go for it as it is something you will NEVER FORGET or REGRET." Now I know what he meant by that, but I did not know it when he told me.

My father was in World War II. He saw and experienced life. He went into the Army, not knowing what his life would be like or if he would ever come home. My father, Ken Smith, whom I am named after, also participated in the military as Private Ken Smith, Queen's Own Cameron Rifles of Winnipeg, Manitoba, when the Canadian forces landed at JUNO BEACH, FRANCE. The number of soldiers who perished was in the thousands, but my father was one of the few who landed on the shores of Juno Beach, which made history and helped change the outcome of WWII.

He did have a near-death experience when he got wounded by a mortar shell that exploded near him, and he got a piece of metal in his back. He went to the hospital in England, got it removed, and went right back to the front line in France.

My Hero, My Best Friend, My Dad!

That being said, I took his advice and had these thoughts embedded in my mind:

- ❖ "Dream what you dare to dream. Go where you want to go. Be what you want to be. "

- ❖ "Accept the challenges so that you may feel the exhalation of victory."
- ❖ "They can, who believe they can."

Knute Rockne is credited with saying, "Leaders are like eagles; they don't flock, and you find them one at a time!" I don't remember where I first heard this quote. I've been in network marketing since I was 19 years old, listened to hundreds of tapes, and attended numerous meetings, rallies, and conventions. I know that you have to step out of your comfort zone, do what others think would be impossible, be different, and be a leader. I've always believed that habits are not taught, they are caught! If this ride inspires others to do something different, out of the normal, and this quote can give them something to relate to, I'm all for it.

That said, I felt a driving spirit to do something different and important in my life that I hoped would make a difference in my grandson's life! Jakob kept me going every day, and at no time did I ever say or feel that this ride, as long as it was going to be, would not happen. When you have that internal passion to make a difference in someone's life, NOTHING will stop you!

WHAT IS A FIREMAN?

He is the guy next door – a man's man with the memory of a little boy,

He has never gotten over the excitement of the engines and sirens and danger.

Yet he stands taller than most of us.

He is a fireman.

He puts it all on the line when the bell rings.

A fireman is at once the most fortunate and the least fortunate of men.

He is a man who saves lives because he has seen too much death.

He is a gentle man because he has seen the awesome power of violence out of control.

He is responsive to children's laughter, because his arms have held too many small bodies that will never laugh again.

He is a man who appreciates the simple pleasures of life:

- Hot coffee held in numb, unbending fingers
- A warm bed for bone and muscle compelled beyond feeling
- The camaraderie of brave men
- the divine peace and selfless service of a job well done in the name of all men.

He doesn't wear buttons, wave flags, or shout obscenities, when he marches, it is to honor a fallen comrade.

He doesn't preach the brotherhood of man,

He LIVES it! ~Author Unknown

My son, Jason, headed out on a call. Jakob & Jason at the station.

THE LIFE OF A FIREFIGHTER

THE ELEPHANT & LIONESS

Whether or not this picture and its associated story is authentic doesn't matter to me. It makes a HUGE statement. You can be the answer to someone in need who can't help themselves. Fear often holds people back, but we can do more than we usually think if we are just willing to step out of our comfort zone. We need to be different because people are always watching and our actions say more than words. So, here is the story:

A lioness and her cub were crossing the savannah, but the heat was excessive, and the cub had great difficulty walking. An elephant realized that the cub would die without help. So, he carried the cub in his trunk beside the mother lioness to a pool of water so that the cub could drink and rest.

 This is how I felt and how it HIT ME when I thought about my grandson, Jakob, and his future. I may be old (older), but when called upon to RIDE FOR JAKOB, I felt like this elephant. I can help carry the load and the burden to help where he cannot help himself. I can walk alongside his mother and father to help support them in putting security in place for Jakob's future. No words can express the feelings and passion I have to help. It will always be a PASSION for me. By giving, you gain. Doing what you can for others and making true connections is the secret to true joy!

HEALTH AND WELLNESS

I once heard this statement, originally by Naomi Judd: "Your body hears everything your mind says."

As I was writing my notes and looking at the past that prepared me for this adventure, I could not overlook the importance of what I did and what I was exposed to early in my youth. I truly believe I ate properly, exercised regularly, took the right supplements, etc., and it allowed me to be in a position (physically) to make this ride. Had I not taken this seriously for several years, I don't think I could have done what I did.

I say that because I have friends who I hadn't seen in years, that when I ran into them later, I was literally shocked, mouth dropping shocked, at the way their bodies had deteriorated and at the level of poor health they exhibited. These people were in my age range, and I grew up in the same environments they did. They were not the same people I knew, which made me realize I took my own health for granted. It also made me start to question: What happened to these friends and why did it affect them so drastically?

As I pondered these questions, I realized that having been exposed to the world of nutritional supplements in my early twenties made the difference. Whatever I was taking and doing, it worked! I saw the reality of how exercise and proper nutrition (supplements) supported a vibrant lifestyle for people of all ages.

Why would I say that? Let me explain...

I worked for the Amway Corporation and started with Amway of Canada Ltd in 1967 when I was 19. When the Nutrilite Corporation merged with Amway, I personally attended the first meeting between the two companies in Ada, Michigan. I was there when the Nutrilite distributors came to the Amway World Headquarters for the first time. I saw and shook hands with these distributors, who were in their 50s, 60s, 70s and even 80s. They were so full of energy and great health that their skin did not show their age or show the usual signs of aging that one would expect. I was amazed at their vitality and outlook on life.

So, what were they doing? What were they taking every day? At first, I thought it had to be some 'drug.' However, as I started to research, I realized that it wasn't a 'drug' but the world of nutrition and supplementation.

You could say I'm from Missouri, the 'show me state.' I'm not, but I did have to see it to believe it. If these people looked that good at their age, walked with energy, and had a 'pep in their step,' so to speak, I wanted that, and I wanted to know how to help others get it. I may have been young - only 21 by this time - but I knew there had to be some wisdom in this stuff.

As I traveled with special guest speakers and doctors over the years, my knowledge about the importance and value of taking supplements increased. I saw so many people have a QUALITY OF LIFE that I envied and wanted. So, I researched the industry and different products to find what I believe is one of the major KEYS (taking vitamin and mineral supplements) to protecting your body's immune system for a higher QUALITY OF LIFE. I will share more of that later.

Then, a friend who was the head of a high school football team visited me, "Ken, get yourself some weights and start an aggressive exercise program." Now, I wasn't a big guy then, and I didn't do a lot of program exercising; but I did spend a lot of time walking and enjoyed the great outdoors, like hunting and fishing. I thought I WAS active. I listened to my friend, bought some weights, and started the Charles Atlas program, on my 30th birthday.

Now, here I am, 40 years later, and I have to say I never stopped exercising or weightlifting. Actually, I got quite aggressive at times and I found my body changing in size, bulk, and energy. I didn't gain a lot of (fat) weight like so many others my age. So, I knew nutritional supplementation and exercise were doing something positive for me.

I found a new interest in swimming, running, and cycling and decided to do a TRIATHLON. I was surprised I could even do it, though I was not a strong swimmer or runner. Then, I decided to enter a few 5K, 10K, ½ marathons. I found that I *could* do them as well. So, I decided to do a few more triathlons.

I have learned to listen to people who prove to be examples of good health. You can tell who to glean from by watching them and then really listening to what they had to share. This is a key life lesson and how you gain WISDOM: LISTEN to those with experience. If you see them walking the walk, whether in business, health, or other areas, and they are obviously successful in whatever field they are engaged in, listen to them!

When I met these people, I always asked, "What do you take/do and why?" If something was evident in their health and lifestyle, I wanted to know more about it. ***Knowledge is the key to me.***

Then, I discovered - WATER! Water, you say, what water? Quality water - highly alkalized mineral water. Why did this appeal to me? I come from a farm background, and my brother-in-law has raised thousands of pigs. One day when I was visiting, I helped him by unloading what I thought were feed bags. As I worked with him, he explained they weren't bags of feed but of MINERALS!

Now, my brother-in-law studied 'animal husbandry' at an agricultural college, he successfully raised pigs for market, and he had done so for a long period of time. Therefore, I knew whatever he shared with me was worth listening to because he had a solid knowledge base from which to glean. He told me pigs are more susceptible to diseases than any other farm animal. IF a pig is to make it to the market and get certification for quality meat, it has to be disease FREE!

To help keep the pigs disease free, there was a very specific process, every person who entered the pig barns went through. I had to change out of my current clothes, shower, and then put on specific barn clothes. We repeated the process: change out of the barn clothes, shower, and put our regular clothes back on. No one was allowed to enter the barns unless they followed this process, because if even one pig got a disease, it would spread to all of them, and the loss would be financially devastating. If my brother-in-law had put so much effort into protecting these pigs' health and determined minerals were also key, I wanted to know more.

So, why the minerals? He told me that certain minerals help the body alkalize the blood. No bacteria, virus, or disease can live in a highly alkalized blood environment. The minerals also oxygenated the blood for better health. I looked at those pigs and the less-than-pristine environment they lived in, yet they *were* indeed healthy. I thought, "Hey, what's suitable for a pig has got to be OK for me too. After all, blood is blood."

That is when I discovered the world of minerals. The right type of minerals: minerals in an ionic form that can quickly be absorbed into your blood and cells. These minerals are taken with water; after all, blood is more than 70% water and is a life source for your health. I found an ionic mineral source and drank at least 2 quarts of water every day. Actually, the rule of thumb is to take your body weight and divide it by 2, and that is how many ounces of water your body needs daily.

What did I find that this did for me? It flushed the toxins, fat, and lactic acid from my body. As I found out, exercise is positive stress and GOOD for you, but it produces lactic acid and causes muscle soreness and cramps. This water flushed that from my muscles and blood, and I had no soreness or cramping after starting this regimen.

I also learned about the interdependence of vitamins and minerals. Your body cannot absorb and utilize vitamins effectively without trace ionic minerals. These minerals increase the absorption of the vitally important vitamins. I figured that if I was spending my hard-earned money on vitamins, I had better invest in a high-quality ionic mineral as well to get the most out of them. Fortunately, getting trace ionic minerals in liquid form is rather inexpensive and easy to find. Because of this, I was able to add them to every water container I drank from.

Something else I heard, read about, and actually saw regarding health and wellness. I talked to a guy who was picking up one of those 'Johnny on the Spot, portable toilets.' I asked him this question: "What are the main things you find in the toilets when you clean them out?" His answer: #1 kid's toys, #2 sanitary napkins, and #3 undigested vitamin/mineral supplements.

What shocked me the most was when he said, "You can still read the labels on most of [the undigested pills]! Can you believe that! People spend good money on supplements that they feel are of good quality, only to have them go right through their digestive system. Wow, to take something and never experience the value promised on the product labels! How discouraging. Because of things like this, I have come to realize that supplements in liquid or powder form appear to get utilized quickly in the body and work better for me. Again, you be the judge on what you feel is best for you.

When talking about health and wellness, supplements, and minerals, you will always be confronted by people who believe they have a good vitamin/mineral supplement. I'm not going to argue with any of them. Each person has to be the judge of what they believe and feel is most beneficial for them. This is what I found over the years to be effective for me.

We live in a 'high-stress' world today. Men and women in the professional fields, labor workers, secretaries, computer system analysts, domestic home engineers, homemakers, etc. Today, any occupation in this fast-paced society is under a lot of stress! That is just the way it is today. The world puts huge demands on the body.

Now add to that the 'athlete' in any professional or recreational sport or just daily exercise - you need to take the best quality supplement you can. Your health must be the most crucial part of your life. It's called QUALITY OF LIFE! You don't think much about it when you're young, but you sure do when you get older.

Just look at the 'baby boomer' generation today. They have the money for security, but they are, in many cases, sick, unhealthy, and cannot even enjoy the lifestyle they worked so hard to achieve. How sad is that?

I am one of those 'baby boomers', but I am not as financially secure as many of them. This is now becoming the largest segment of the baby boomer generation. Once financially set, they now find themselves unable to retire due to bankruptcy, downsizing, foreclosure, and bad investments. They have to work and cannot get sick. If ever there was a group of people who wished for a promising, healthy future they could depend on, it is now!

Here I am now, enjoying a healthy lifestyle that people notice and ask questions about. How did I ride my bike 3502 miles from the Pacific to the Atlantic Ocean? How did I go for 56 days on my bike, 6 to 8 hours a day, and sometimes longer? How did I do this without PAIN, SORENESS, and FATIGUE issues at my age?

My answer: this lifestyle. It has proven that the WISDOM I gleaned about nutrition and health over the years was the right thing to do, despite how crazy some people thought it was. I feel so grateful that I listened to them and now have the QUALITY OF LIFE I always dreamed possible.

MANNATECH

Mannatech is the network marketing company that provided me with its products and supported this ride. After years of research and experience, I know the importance of good nutrition. Therefore, I knew I needed to feed and fortify my body daily with the correct supplementation if this ride was going to be successful.

As mentioned in the previous section, I had competed in a few marathons and even triathlons before this ride. However, I was younger, and the demand on my body was short-lived. The average marathon is around 4½ to 5 hours long. This ride would be for approximately 2 months! Day after day, 8-10 hours daily, with only a few rest days between. If you've read through my journal entries, you know that some days, I rode 90+ miles in a day.

I knew I needed supplements that WORKED, or this ride would end prematurely, which was unacceptable. Through a series of events, I was referred to a company called Mannatech. I went to their website and began my research. From the product information and research studies on their website, I was very confident I would experience the results they indicated. I believe that when a network marketing company develops, produces, and markets any product (nutrition is just one of them), it has to be of good quality, tested, and effective, or the company would not exist or be successful. As I said, I chose Mannatech based on my research at the time.

I reach out to them, and they offered to provide all of the supplements of my choice in exchange for an honest review. I realize many of you don't know me personally, but I want to state up front that what I report here is 100% authentic and from my personal experience. I have not been compensated by Mannatech or anyone associated with this company for my review of these products.

Based on ACTUAL daily product performance OVER 56 DAYS of extreme physical conditions, intense heat, rough terrain, energy drain, weather changes, and the mental demand of such a journey - the Mannatech products with 'glyconutrient' nutrient formulation performed beyond expectation. I was mentally and physically stronger when I reached the Atlantic. The only thing I can attribute to this being possible is the nutritional supplements Mannatech provided me throughout my trip.

This was not a 'one-day' or 'one-week' test but 'two months of daily demand' test! I am sure there are other products that people have researched and used that have seen beneficial results. I am not here to judge other nutritional supplements. Mannatech offered to supply my supplemental needs for this ride across the U.S. from coast to coast, and I thank them for believing in me.

Before taking these supplements, I ALWAYS felt the soreness and effects after an aggressive workout, sometimes even hours later into the following day. While taking these supplements, even at the age of 70, I had no muscle soreness, cramps, or fatigue from the intense demand on my body during the entire ride - NOTHING!

It is only right for me to explain that hydration is a key factor for me, so I made sure to consume as much alkalized mineral water as possible throughout the day. (If you have not read the Health and Wellness section, this mineralized water is explained there.) I had to consume more water and have a greater intake of energy supplements. Other than the alkaline mineral water, the only other supplements I took were the Mannatech products: Ambrotose Life, Empact+, and TruPlenish.

Ambrotose Life is a nutritional supplement that promotes the immune system, gastrointestinal health, and cognitive function. I took the recommended amount twice daily: once before we left and at the end of the day's ride.

Empact+ is designed for endurance, hydration, and recovery. I knew that my body needed more than just water for the long riding days and especially the hot temperatures. Empact+ was a safe and delicious way to keep my body hydrated due to the daily physical activity and strain I put on it and all my muscles. It performed beyond expectation.

TruPlenish is a protein shake filled with vitamins, minerals, probiotics, Glyconutrients, and over 20 grams of protein. I knew my body needed more protein to function at such a high demand, so I made one of these daily shakes.

My first day of riding was 58 miles, and I pushed my bike up mountain hills for 8 + hours. Remember, before this, I had only had one ride with my bike for a total of 20 miles. This was a very aggressive day of exercise, and only the first day of really pushing my body to the MAX! I was expecting muscle cramps, soreness, and fatigue by the end of the day, like I experienced before, but it didn't happen. I went to bed expecting to be almost crippled from the intensity of the previous day's work out, but it didn't happen. I woke up with NO PAIN, NO SORENESS, NO STIFFNESS - SOMETHING WAS DEFINITELY DIFFERENT!

Whether it was my first day, my fifth day, or my twenty-fifth day, the performance results were the same: NO PAIN, NO SORENESS, NO STIFFNESS. It's tough for me to put into words how I felt when I actually saw the Atlantic Ocean. I was at the end of this epic journey and I wasn't crawling the last few feet or struggling to make it to the finish. I was healthy, energetic, and mentally strong.

It *was* a very emotional moment with a HUGE feeling of WOW, I actually did this!

After my ride, Mannatech invited me to fly to Dallas, TX, and be a featured speaker on their Tuesday Night Live program. I shared the effect of Ambrotose Life, Empact+, and TruPlenish on my body during and after my RIDE FOR JAKOB.

If I had failed to complete this ride (which was not an option), then I would have failed Jakob. Having a mindset and attitude of "I can or will do this plus what my body needs to sustain the demand I had to have" were two major components for success. I had to share what effect I experienced in using the Mannatech products on my ride. I will leave you with this - these products WORK!

When asked, "Would you do another ride like this again?" My answer is ABSOLUTELY, with Mannatech products on board! I know this, and I will continue to use these products. Why? The proof was in the performance, hands down.

The most significant testimony from this journey is that with the help of the Mannatech supplements, not only did I do this amazing thing at the age of 70, but I did it and came out stronger emotionally, physically, and mentally. Many others may ride the trails from coast to coast, and I encountered many of them, but in my conversations, NONE experienced the strengthening I did, which can only be attributed to Mannatech.

ABOUT THE AUTHOR

This book has hopefully been designed to inspire you (the reader) to reach your potential to "go for the top." Along this journey, I hope you are encouraged to reach out to others to empower them to be the BEST they can be. All while recognizing and giving thanks to GOD for who you are and what example to others, young and old, can be accomplished IF you believe in yourself.

So then - who is KEN SMITH? Let me briefly overview my past and how it prepared me for my RIDE FOR JAKOB.

I am a RISK taker!

I like to live on the edge of a new adventure, no matter what it is - business, health, or spiritual understanding. I'm always asking, 'what can I do to get to the next level that will take me to the edge of my comfort zone!' I want to experience anything that will challenge me physically and emotionally and take me to limits that are hard to explain but can inspire others to say, "If he can do it, so can I." I've had a lot of scary incidents in my life, but if the risk factor was a little higher than usual, that's what made it all the more interesting!

I love LIFE!

I like meeting new people.

If there is a statement that will give you an idea or feeling of who I am, it would be this quote that I have come to live by: FIND SOMETHING - BIGGER THAN YOURSELF!

My father taught me to be a 'fighter', never give up, play hard, work hard, and regardless of the JOB, take it on. The only way you gain experience is through failure; the more you keep trying, the more you succeed. Then, when you give advice or counsel, it is advice that is valuable because you lived through it.

At 17, my grandfather enrolled me in the Jr. Forest Ranger program. I left home for the first time and went to work at a camp in the remote Canadian North Country. For four months, I helped build bridges for the road crew in case of future forest fires. This was an experience I will never forget, and to this day, I still go on a family fishing trip to the lake in this area—very remote and mostly unchanged.

At the age of 19, I started with Amway of Canada. I was the 13th employee and I started my education in network marketing as a stock boy in the warehouse processing orders.

I watched men and women from all ethnicities and ages, some professionals, but most just ordinary people who wanted something better for their family and future. I watched as they bought in to the value of having their own business—something they could do alongside what they did 9-5 to pay the bills. I watched as they built something no one could take away from them and where no one else controlled their income.

Watching all this embedded in my mind that anyone, even me, could achieve our dreams IF prepared to work, follow a system, and be taught the necessary skills.

Through the advice of an Amway distributor, I enrolled in the Dale Carnegie Course. I will say that this forced me to change my way of thinking, took me out of my comfort zone, and enabled me to believe I could change my circumstances. I could have the career I wanted, be the person I wanted to be, and get out of my introverted, shy way of thinking. It literally changed my life and made me the risk taker I have become today.

I became the Amway product expert on ALL the products. Distributors at all levels sought me out to ask questions and wanted MY advice. Opportunities began to be presented to me in the corporate world. Do I have the intellectual/educational skills needed for these positions? No! But I did have the I CAN DO IT ATTITUDE and approach to life.

Now came my BIGGEST FEAR! Public speaking. I could answer the phone, I could write a letter, I could give a tour, BUT speak in public to a large group, NO! Especially not to distributors who – in my mind – were more qualified than I was. I couldn't do it! So, what happened?

I was asked to be a special guest company speaker at a local meeting. They didn't ask me to discuss the products; they wanted me to present the Sales and Marketing Plan. What! I'd never done that before, and I didn't even know where to start; BUT I agreed. I CAN DO THIS!

Talk about scared. The meeting was at a local college in a lecture room, and there were about 50 people present, most from Canada and some from the US. I went to the stage wearing my new suit like armor and was introduced as an expert from Amway.

I looked at the audience, opened my mouth to start talking as I drew the marketing circles on the white board, and FROZE! I couldn't think of anything I was supposed to write or present. I couldn't even speak. I turned and just left the stage. All I heard as I went was - who is this IDIOT. It literally destroyed my confidence and it took all my willpower to hold back the tears. My wife was there, and she even asked, "What happened?" I WILL NEVER FORGET THAT DAY.

I decided never to accept another speaking engagement, but my life as a speaker was not over. A few months later, the GM of Amway of Canada and I had to do a 5-day speaking tour across Western Canada. *MY* job and responsibility was to do a few product demonstrations that I was comfortable with. The GM was the Master of Ceremonies and did all introductions. Well, guess what happened?

One day, just a few minutes before the start of the meeting, I got a call. With over 500 distributors in attendance, the GM told me over the phone that I had to open the meeting because he would not be able to be there. I had to start everything, make the announcements, introduce the speakers, and make my presentation until he arrived.

I knew then that my future was at stake; I had to do this! Somehow, I did, and it went well. Did I make mistakes, absolutely, but people came up to me afterwards. "You did a great job." "Well done." Even the GM said, "I am proud of you!"

I realized later that he was always there. He set me up, but he knew I could do it. That was the beginning of my public speaking career. The largest group I have spoken to was in Rio de Janeiro, Brazil. In my capacity as the new President and General Manager for Amway do Brasil, I spoke to 23,000 excited Portuguese distributors.

Fear is just a feeling you create in your mind. Now I get excited about risk and adventure, knowing the fear of disaster or failure is there, but I thrive on it. What's around the next corner? Who am I going to meet? What difficulty will I be confronted with that will enable me to grow and be an example for others?

Each person has to choose what they want to engage in, and I am not here to judge any company or person. That being said, the network marketing industry can and will change you in many ways. I admire all network marketing corporations because they offer anyone the ability to change their lives and future IF they want to. It instilled in me the idea that I can do whatever I set my mind to do. I am the only thing that genuinely holds me back from creating the future I truly want for myself and my family. Under God, my future was totally up to me. I would be the MASTER OF MY DESTINY AND FUTURE.

Here is what I discovered along my network marketing journey:

- You become a different person
- The person GOD created you to be
- The person you *really* want to be
- Free from stress
- Free from worry
- You take risks
- You step out of your comfort zone
- A person who spends more quality time with others and their family
- Your health and quality of life will become more important than when you were younger.

Some may say that this mindset is not very 'Christian.' However, I believe that God is the one who created us and He gave us the breath to live life. I also believe that God is alive and living in me, and because I have chosen to follow Him, He actively guides my path. Therefore, the desires of my heart will align with His will for me and my family because we have chosen to follow after Him. So, everything I have revealed assumes that God is at the center guiding my choices.

It is amazing how harsh words stay with you all of your life. When I was younger, I was told some very negative things. In reaction to those statements echoing within me, I decided early in my life that I would SHOW THE WORLD, SHOW MY FAMILY, and SHOW MY CHILDREN that their father is someone they can depend on FOREVER! But life is not always easy or predictable.

As mentioned, I became the first GM and President of Amway Brazil. This came about after I was told that my position in Canada was no longer available. Essentially, I lost my job but was told I could go to another country for two years. This meant I had to break the news to my entire family, that we either left everything we were accustomed to, family, friends, language, culture, and lifestyle, or I became unemployed and had to find another way to support us. Stressful.

What did I do? I took my family, all of them, to live in a foreign country to experience a different lifestyle and culture. Moving alone added a lot of pressure and stress, but then we realized that no one spoke English other than the employees at the company! My family had to learn how to live in a totally Portuguese, and sometimes hostile, environment without knowing how to speak the language.

Shortly after we moved to Brazil, my father died, and my oldest son's dog was poisoned, after which he decided to go back to Canada. Now my family is grieving and divided - another layer of stress.

All of this happened in a very short period of time while I was trying to run a new international company that was exploding with growth. Generally, that would be great news, but then I experience an abduction attempt at gunpoint, putting my life in danger.

When my two years in Brazil were over, my family and I moved to Grand Rapids, Michigan. Shortly after our return to the U.S., I made a bad financial decision, and left the company after 32 years of being with them.

My wife and I decided to start with a new company, and in the first 1½ years, I lost my job due to corporate downsizing. I had to declare bankruptcy, something I never would have imagined myself having to do, and we lost our house due to foreclosure.

Why am I sharing all of this with you? What is the point?

Life is constantly stressful. Family is important; strive never to let them down. Never give up, no matter the challenges you face. Be strong, a fighter, a risk taker, and yet gentle. Protect your family and never hurt them.

My father always said, "Outwork everyone, be an example, never give up, never back down, and respect women, especially your mother." I've worked hard from early in my life and learned to respect older people. These are good things to live by that created the person I am today and that I hope to pass on to the next generation.

My life has been a roller coaster of experiences and emotions at times. Through them all I have come to believe that we should "Not only follow your DREAM but CHASE after your DREAM!" Whatever dreams you have.

You only have one life, live it to the fullest and impact as many as you can with your living example. People watch you always. You don't always have to say much, if anything, but the way you live and what you do (ACTION) not only touch others, but gives them the motivation to change their own lives, if they want to change. We can be free from stress and worry and become the person who pays more attention to family, others, health, and the future with the GOAL to create a QUALITY OF LIFE.

Though not all of my experiences have been pleasant, I have had the opportunity to do just that – LIVE A QUALITY LIFE. Probably the most significant adventure that came because of my Brazilian experience was going to the Amazon rainforest under special authorization of the Brazilian authorities to enter the Amazon. Most people will never be allowed to enter the areas I visited, and experience the things that I did, most of them you couldn't even imagine were possible. There have been three times in my life that I actually thought I was going to die - two of those times were in the Amazon. I will never forget the snakes, bugs, mosquitoes, piranha, jaguars, caimans, scorpions, malaria, all very real and experienced firsthand.

Throughout my quest for a quality life, I have traveled to the Mayan temples, Alaska, the Yukon, and the Canadian north to James Bay. I have also gone whitewater rafting down rivers in West Virginia, Pennsylvania, and through the Grand Canyon. I have sailed in tall ships through the Mediterranean and Caribbean. I have deep-sea fished in Florida and Guatemala. I have traveled through Panama, Costa Rica, Honduras, Mexico, not to mention Guam, the Philippines, and Japan. I have traveled to 9 Canadian provinces, both territories, and most of the United States.

Travel, taking risks, and doing things that most people only dream about excites me. I have done four triathlons, a Tough Mudder endurance challenge, various marathons previously mentioned, rappelled down a mountain, and had many more incredible experiences.

My bucket list is still extensive and I still hope to be able to fulfill every one of them: I want to do an Iron Man event, walk to the North Pole, climb Mt. Kilimanjaro in Africa, ride my bike across Canada from the West Coast to the East Coast, and then ride from the Pacific to the Atlantic, starting in San Diego, California, and ending in Key West, Florida. For the first time, after my experience with Mannatech and my RIDE FOR JAKOB, I believe all these are possible without a significant cost to my body.

Taking on this decision to ride my bike from Seaside, Oregon, to Revere Beach, Massachusetts (near Boston) was first on my bucket list, but in addition, I wanted to experience the challenge, the test of endurance, the obstacles and risks that were going to happen. The thrill of this adventure excited me every day; what would I experience today, what would the next corner reveal, what new memory would I have, and what new story could I pass on to my children and grandchildren? I wanted to do something that made a difference, that would make a statement, and something my children, grandchildren, and wife would remember about their father, grandfather, and husband.

"I wanted to do something bigger than myself." And I DID!

Interview, Message, and the Why of my Experience

- I had an incredible feeling of accomplishment riding my bike from the Pacific Ocean to the Atlantic Ocean.
- I had a DREAM of doing this at some point in my life, but it did not happen until a BIG WHY appeared.
- I knew I could actually live my DREAM - AWAKE! And experience it every day.
- I read this statement once that said: 'You can't believe in a dream until you can believe in you (and that your dream is possible).'
- The WHY has to give you goosebumps every time you think about it, and that REASON or WHY has to be so strong that it just DRIVES you every day.
- JAKOB was my WHY – my REASON - My grandson!
- It did not matter what the challenges, issues, circumstances, or obstacles developed each day – I faced them and dealt with them as they developed. I fully believe doing this develops your CHARACTER and the person you become.
- Having a GOAL is important, but there is always a beginning and an end to a goal.
- To me, a goal is simply a JOURNEY.
- It's how you take the journey that makes all the difference

- Enjoy it because:
  - You might not have another opportunity to experience this dream again.
  - This particular journey will be so different from any other that you engage in, and you will miss valuable memories that could have not only impacted your life but the lives of many others.
- Your ACTIONS say so many things to so many people.
- It's not always what you say that counts, but it is WHAT YOU DO!
- It is this ACTION that will have an impact on others, and you could have NO IDEA that what you DID meant anything to them.
- Let me give you a few examples:
  - I met this young woman along the trail somewhere in New York. I met her and a couple of others, and they asked, "Who is Jakob?" So, I told the story of why I was making this RIDE FOR JAKOB.

    I gave each of them my flyer handout which had my contact information. Here is what she texted me: "Hello, I just met you, and I know this is probably weird, but you just made my life so much better and helped me. I will never think I have it bad or complain about my life and take it for granted because that could have been me; if there is anything I can do to help, let me know."

- I got this message from a man: I saw the news report about your journey from Albany, NY. I was completely touched and moved by your cause. I saw you today, but you were busy in a bike shop, and I didn't want to interrupt you. I just wanted to shake your hand and give you some water. Prayers for you and your family. I wanted to tell you that I had a very dedicated grandfather like yourself at one time. Thank you for inspiring me.

- Here is another example of 'what you do can leave an impression on others.' This was another rider that I met while resting on the trail.

He was 6'8" tall and 45 years old. He told me he rides 75 to 80 miles every day when he does a long ride across the county. He was obviously bigger and stronger, and it was obvious how he could do that kind of distance every day—he was just stronger and had more power.

When I met him, I had already done 40 miles and would only go another 10 to the city I had chosen for the day. He stated that his destination was Albany, and that was another 40 miles yet to travel. I told him I would like to ride with him for at least another 10 miles, if I could keep up with him. I was comfortable riding 60 miles each day if necessary.

So, we rode together for the next 10 miles, but I decided to go another 10 miles at least. We stopped for a short break, and he wanted to keep going for another 20 miles. Doing that meant I would go a total of 80 plus miles.

I thought, "What's another 20 miles," and we carried on. At 80 miles, he said, "I can't believe you kept up with me, especially at your age." I had already been cycling for over 50 days at that time. I don't know what it was that made me do the extra 30 to 40 miles. Maybe it was pride or just plain 'I can do this' attitude. But I do know this - YOU can push yourself, and you can do more! Regardless of the circumstances or even if you are tired.

I was tired but not exhausted. At the end of the day, I just felt good about myself, and I knew that no matter what issues may develop, I can face them with drive, determination, and the attitude that I CAN DO THIS!

AND, believe me, more testing was still to come.

- Berkshires - 7 miles of walking my bike uphill for over 4 hours, pushing a weight of some 100 lbs., bike and gear.
- Fog - rain
- Heavy traffic

When times got hard, I found that I fully believed someone was watching over me. Someone always seemed to show up when not expected or right after I prayed and asked for help. It was amazing the number of times when an answer to prayer was fulfilled. At times, I did not recognize it till much later, and then it hit me, "Wow, that is exactly what I asked for." I don't know how to explain it, but it happened! As I mentioned, people watch you, and your actions say a lot. That is what gets embedded in your mind forever (you don't forget personal fulfillment). It does something to you.

- how you live
- how you think
- how you approach life
- how you approach challenges
- how you treat other people
- how you face adversity
- how it develops your character
- how it develops your - I CAN DO THIS, attitude

People watch you:

- older people watch you

- younger people watch you
- kids watch you
- athletes watch you
- businessmen and women watch you

WHY?

- you are different
- you stand out
- you have a 'can do it attitude'
- you take RISKS
- you become an example for others, and you touch people in so many ways that you don't know about them.

WHAT AN AWESOME FEELING…AND then you think - what's my next adventure? And you start the process of DREAMING all over again!

Regardless of what other people think about you, don't worry about it. Just have a "just do it" approach to life.

- that will keep you young

- that keeps you active
- that keeps your mind in an active mindset
- Age doesn't mean aging - it's just a number

I have always had a 'get out the way' attitude. That doesn't mean you are bragging about what you can do or what you did. You just know in your knower that you have a 'can do it approach to life.' I want to feel that I have touched others and hopefully encourage them to make a change in their life if they want to change. How can I touch someone's life today?

So, my driving force was my grandson, JAKOB. How can I make a difference in his life! I believe he will know some day, but if he never does - I will know and I will be fulfilled. I read once that 'when you see others succeed - you are FULFILLED!'

Habits are not TAUGHT - they are CAUGHT!

I have also come to realize that you should never think that your life couldn't change at any time and you'd have to face the unexpected. To me, my family is of the greatest importance, and having a wife who not only stands by your side, regardless of circumstances, is a gift that you hold onto and cherish.

As I was reading these notes and experiences, they touched my heart all over again. I believe that no matter what you do in life, you need to hold onto the LOVE you have with all of your family and friends. My wife, Jan, and my daughter, Kimberley, passed away in October 2021, just 20 days apart, both from breast cancer. Until someone you love is gone, you don't realize the true meaning of spending as many precious moments as you are allowed before they slip by.

Things like the time you took for granted, that life is good, and thinking it is just another day are concepts we disregard. In reality, each and every day is a PRECIOUS GIFT that GOD has given you to appreciate. Until something or someone is gone, what it means to reach out and touch as many people as you can does not become a reality. When you finally realize you will not have the chance again to have those moments with them because they are gone, it impacts you.

BLESSINGS

Below is a list of a few of the many blessings I encountered during my journey.

- Mass - bike shop surprise - 12 miles out (2 broken spokes, fender guard loose, all hex nuts loose

- Rochester - 2 guys through the city after prayer
- Syracuse - father/son through the city after prayer
- Schenectady - guy I met on the trail - prayer
- Accidents: logging truck - guard rail - Erie canal
- Fall off the bike 4 times
- No aches, no pain
- People who donated - 85%--son, daughter, brother, sister, or someone in the family
- Bernie - my flag in his window, the owner of the Quality Motel - FREE room
- Heat stroke - no water, no shade, 113 degrees (military man)
- No water, people just showed up after prayer + water sign
- Summit no food that night, but meal shaker, but FREE room
- Women in a pickup truck - fence lady - why are you here?
- Bull story
- Flat tire - steel belt metal (from interstate highway, some miles away from the motel)
- Friend gave me his hat, a strobe light, and a reflective vest
- Police escort into town - they were looking for us

- Blessed with housing - Portland fire dept - Orofino - Umatilla - Minnesota
- Idaho pass - catholic priest - near accident - took me down the highway 5 miles
- Newspaper interviews
- People paying for lunch because they saw my newspaper article or on TV
- Fruit stand in Fargo, free food
- Cross on road—Chris's financial blessing—plus the other guys saw the cross but did not stop to pick it up; it was meant for me!
- Grand Rapids: Fox 17, channels 8 and 13, and WKTV
- London, CFPL radio –Mike Stubs interview
- Albany (Albion) drive by
- Mannatech (Revere beach)
- My son, daughter, and grandson showing up
- My sister Lois and Roger showing up
- Farmer providing water when I needed it - the only person along the highway
- Praying and someone appearing to help me
- Needed a new chain and clip-on shoe (the bike shop was just there on a corner in that town)

- Call from a TV network in Bismarck, ND - who heard about my ride
- Post office in Hebron, a tiny town (4 bags too heavy), the post office right next to the restaurant was totally unexpected, but an answer to prayer as I really needed to downsize + donate
- Dog ran out barking and stopped me on the trail - women came out to save me and donated
- Fargo, ND - TV live interview
- Food paid for in Mass. Bakeshop and breakfast outlet + donated $100
- Text messages - the effect it had on others (read)
- Dennis cooking, camping, food, 33 degrees
- Dennis opened his home for us to stay for two nights
- Great Falls, MT - RV people - food, sleeping accommodations
- Rides: Dean of Vet WSU Rogers Pass
- A lady from Medora/Bismarck found it hard to ride to Quality Inn and wanted me to share with her children what my ride was all about!

STRUGGLES

- I felt alone - no houses, no farms, you feel totally helpless many times
- 20 days over 100 degrees of heat
- 8 % downgrade-38 mph - crosswind - hands numb
- No water - no shade
- Long rolling hills, mountains very steep (had to walk them)
- Berkshire mountains are very hard to cross - 7 miles uphill pushing a bike of 100 lbs in the rain)
- No cell coverage - I felt alone many times, with no houses, no farms, and no traffic to flag down, I felt totally helpless many times
- No shoulders on the road (not friendly to ride on)
- NO turning back, nowhere to go, but keep going every day
- 4 - 6 - 8 % downhill grades
- 3 hills: 2 at 4 miles long, one at 7 miles long, and six at 4 miles long - pushing and walking in shoes not designed for walking but riding.

Thank You and Appreciation

I cannot finish this book without expressing my thoughts and feelings of love, thanks, and gratitude for all of the encouragement and daily prayers, which gave me the strength to fulfill a personal dream and to live that dream awake every day.

My RIDE FOR JAKOB was such a wonderful experience, not only for me personally but also for my grandson and his family!

My biggest THANK YOU goes out to my grandson, JAKOB. Every day, Jakob inspired me to push through ALL the daily challenges. Without you and your picture with me daily, this ride would have meant very little. Yes, I got a personal sense of satisfaction and accomplishment from completing the ride, but it was YOU who inspired me, motivated me, and drove me every day to do what some would say was impossible, especially at the age of 70. Love you JAKIE!

My second biggest goes to my wife for enduring while I was gone. I wish you were here to see this book come to fruition, but I know one day I'll see you again and we can celebrate then. THANK YOU, JAN - I LOVE YOU!

I want to say a BIG THANK YOU to MANNATECH for believing in me and providing all the products and supplements for this ride. Your support went beyond a product test. A special shout out to SONNA, who met me along the way and at the Atlantic.

ANOTHER BIG THANK YOU goes out to Fire Marshall Bill Smith, the Chiefs, and those in Grand Rapids who supported me and the RIDE FOR JAKOB. Without your letter of support, the many connections across the nation would not have been possible.

My sincere THANKS and appreciation goes to the Fire Fighter Association both here in the U.S. and Canada. The firefighters and stations not only opened their doors to provide a room for the night, plus food and fellowship but also for their wonderful expression of love for Jakob and my firefighter son, Jason Smith, by their donations for Jakob's future and security.

This was another expression of what this profession does for special needs children and special causes, and the support it has for its fellow firefighters. Words cannot express my thanks for their support. Even though my physical RIDE FOR JAKOB is over, I will continue to 'Ride for Jakob' every day I have left. Thank you ALL so much!

A HEARTFELT thanks to Jakob's mother, Sue Smith. As I was looking at the Facebook site, www.facebook.com/rideforjake, I could not help but see the number of pictures and all the comments that came from the postings of these pictures. Throughout my trip, you did an amazing job of staying in contact with me and reporting my progress. I could never have been able to provide all those following me on the RIDE FOR JAKOB with these daily updates without her expertise and creative skills. Thank you so much, Sue; you made this journey one that everyone could identify with and created excitement for my ride. I so appreciate you and love you!

The Facebook page is no longer active, but you can find some posts if you search 'Ride for Jakob' or 'Ken Smith.' Many videos and interviews are available on YouTube.

Jakob is so loved by his sister, Brooklynn. Thank you so much for your love and caring spirit for your brother and for allowing me to use the incredible poem you wrote for your classmates (shared in Part 1 of this book), which says it all. Jakob is so blessed to have a sister like you. Love YOU!

My sister, Lois, and brother-in-law, Roger, were with me daily as I took this journey along with many of their friends who also helped. Having her as my 'eyes in the sky' gave me that sense of security all along the way. THANK YOU so much.

To my daughter, Kyra Jacobs, who was also on my 'eyes in the sky' team, your check-ins not only made me laugh at times but showed me how much you care about me. The assurance that someone would know if something happened gave me the peace to keep journeying. You're awesome, THANK YOU, and I love you, Kyra!

A special thank you to Dennis Blackburn, a good friend and previous co-worker at SATIC. Meeting us at Lola Pass and opening your home to us for some additional rest was a true blessing. THANK YOU for all your support. Your visit meant the world.

Words cannot express my gratitude for Chris Cuvar, my best friend. This ride would not have been possible had it not been for your support, my friend! You knew that Jan wanted me to do this RIDE FOR JAKOB and encouraged me to follow this dream. With her cancer and being quite sick, it was difficult for me to agree. However, you stepped in with your medical background, firefighter and paramedic training, and offered to take care of her while I was gone. Just knowing you would be there, checking in with Jan on a daily basis, gave me so much peace. I knew my wife was in good hands. THANK YOU for all you have done not only during this ride but also for helping us fight Jan's cancer for over 6 years! Words of APPRECIATION seem deficient to express the depth of meaning of your many texts, prayers along the way, your personal visit in Flint, and all the help you've given me since. Your input on this book has been paramount to its completion. THANK YOU, my friend!

To ALL of my family, but especially those who drove so far to be a part of the various events along this journey, I will never forget when I showed up, and you were there to greet me. I heard a DAD make this statement - he said: "If your dad can live out his DREAM - then nothing is impossible for you (his children).

And so, I believe - if your grandpa can live out his DREAM - then NOTHING is IMPOSSIBLE for you (my grandchildren).

THANK YOU to those who have followed, prayed for me, and donated during my RIDE FOR JAKOB.

A final THANK YOU goes to Melanie Schlatter and Dot's House! Melanie came into our family through her friendship with my daughter, Kimberley, back in 1999. We fell in love with her and adopted her into our family without hesitation. I knew she had written a book before, so when I was ready to publish RIDE FOR JAKOB, I reached out to her. Without the personal touches and help on this book, it would never have happened, let alone been such an awesome book! Love you, Kiddo!

My goal is still to help Jakob secure his future.

Profits from the sale of this book will go to Jakob's Fund. If you have questions, please reach out to Ken Smith at kensmithconnections@gmail.com

To make a donation, scan our QR code

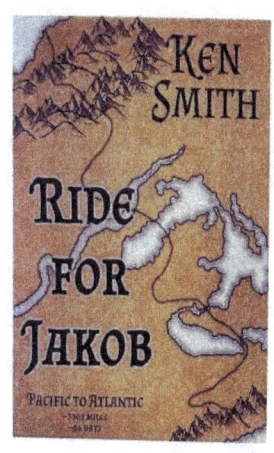

To order a book
RIDE FOR JACOB

Or visit
https://dots-house-store.square.site/product/ride-for-jakob/36

Lebanon, Kansas, USA
www.dotsmicropublishinghouse.com

www.ingramcontent.com/pod-product-compliance
Lightning Source LLC
Chambersburg PA
CBHW051940290426
44110CB00015B/2053